You Are Unstoppable

A Study Guide Companion to the Audiobook

Practical Principles for Overcoming Setbacks and Experiencing Breakthroughs

Mike Prah

ISBN: 979-8-218-20760-1 (Audiobook Companion Paperback)
ISBN: 979-8-218-20761-8 (Audiobook Companion Ebook)
ISBN: 978-1-662-868-474 (Main Book Hardcover
ISBN: 978-1-662-868-467 (Main Book Paperback)
ISBN: 978-1-662-868-481 (Main Ebook)

Contents

Part One:Discussion Questions for Reflection or Small Group Bible Study...1

Chapter 1—Living the Overflowing Life 2

Chapter 2—Turning Setbacks into Success...............................9

Chapter 3—How to See Your Dreams Become a Reality.........18

Chapter 4—How to Overcome the Enemy Within...................28

Chapter 5—How to Be Confident and Victorious in Crisis 37

Chapter 6—How to Break Free from Strongholds...................47

Chapter 7—What It Takes to Be a Great Leader—The 8 cs of Influential Leadership 58

Chapter 8—How to Live a Life of Significance.........................70

Chapter 9—How to Overcome Your Weakness to Become a Stronger Person 77

Chapter 10— How to Recover From Your Hurts.......................86

Part Two..95

Small Group Guidelines and Helpful Hints for Hosts.................95

Small Group Guidelines 96

Helpful Tips for Small Group Hosts 98

My Small Group Rooster...102

Connect with Mike Prah 103

Additional Notes..104

Additional Notes..105

Additional Notes..106

Part One:
Discussion Questions for Reflection or Small Group Bible Study

Chapter 1—Living the Overflowing Life

Using This Discussion Guide

- This is only a guide. This discussion guide contains too many questions for most groups to answer in a single session. You may choose a few questions from each section after considering the needs of your group.

A. OPEN YOUR SESSION WITH PRAYER

B. INTRODUCTION:

This Bible discussion will explore the keys to experiencing the overflowing life. God desires to take you from an overwhelmed life to an overflowing life! Instead of a scarcity mindset, God wants you to have a surplus mindset because He is more than enough to meet all your needs and everyone else's. Fear, worry, envy, resentment, and insecurity result from a scarcity mindset and an overwhelmed life. A surplus mindset and overflowing life result in contentment, peace, and security.

C. BIBLE DISCUSSION:

SECTION 1: PERSONALIZING THE MESSAGE

a) What parts of the message stood out the most to you, and why?

b) What did the message say to you that gave you hope, encouragement, or comfort?

c) What did you read that made you think differently about something or that led to a sense of conviction?

d) How did the message make you more grateful to God the Father or Jesus Christ?

e) What positive result could occur from putting into practice the message or the painful consequences of ignoring it?

SECTION 2: DIGGING DEEPER

At the beginning of this chapter, Mike quotes a definition of F–O–M–O (Fear of Missing Out) as "The uneasy and sometimes all-consuming feeling that you are missing out—that your peers are doing, in the know about, or in possession of more or something better than you." Under this framing, nearly 75% of people say they struggle with FOMO. Mike suggests that because of the desire to keep up with everybody, people have overbooked their calendars, overspent their money, overloaded their emotions, overcrowded their days, overvalued other people's approval, and overlooked the Lord. As a result, people are overstressed, overanxious, and overwhelmed.

• Why do you think FOMO has such a strong influence on people?

• What impact has the fear of missing out (FOMO) had on you or someone you know?

Scarcity Vs. Surplus Mindset

Mike notes that someone with a scarcity mindset believes there is a limited amount of resources in the world, and if some people have more, then they will have less. God's infinite power, goodness, and grace are central to the surplus mentality, so I can rest assured that He will provide for my needs and everyone else's.

- Which of these viewpoints does God want you to have—A scarcity or Surplus mindset?
- What are the implications of holding on to each of these mindsets?

Philippians 4:19: "You can be sure that God will supply everything you need from His abundant wealth that He pours out on us from Jesus Christ" (MSG+GN).

- What do you notice about this verse? What words or ideas jump out to you?
- What do you think the main message is?
- In what ways could you make use of the message from Philippians 4:19?

John 7:37-38: "On the last day of the festival, Jesus stood and shouted to the crowds: 'If you are thirsty, COME TO ME and drink! Everyone who REALLY BELIEVES IN ME will have rivers of living water FLOWING OUT OF THEIR LIVES" (NLT).

What does Jesus say is necessary to tap into God's overflowing life according to John 7:37-3[1]

Isaiah 48:17-18: "I am the holy God who rescues you. For your own good, I teach you and lead you along the right path. How I wish that you had obeyed my commands! Then your success and good fortune would have OVERFLOWED like a flooding river!" (CEV).

- According to Isaiah 48:17-18, how does God describe the overflowing life? And how can we receive it?[2]

---

[1] "Come to Me," and "really believes in Me."
[2] Isaiah 48:17-18. Overflowing life = "flooding river." By receiving God's teachings, following His leading, and obey His commands.

- What do you think the main message of this Scripture is?
- What is God trying to tell you through this Scripture passage?

HOW TO LIVE THE OVERFLOWING LIFE
1. STAY CONNECTED TO JESUS EVERY DAY

John 15:5: Jesus: "I am the vine, and you are the branches. If you stay joined to me ... you will produce lots of fruit. But you cannot do anything without me" (CEV).

John 15:7-11: Jesus: "If you stay connected to me and my words remain in you, you may ask any request you like, and it will be granted! My true disciples produce much fruit. This brings glory to my Father . . . So, stay connected to my love. You stay connected to my love when you obey me . . . I've told you this so that you'll be filled with my joy. Yes, your cup of joy will OVERFLOW!" (NLT+LB).

- What phrases or thoughts jump out at you as you read John 15:5 and 15:7-11?
- In John 15:7-11, Jesus lists four beneficial reasons for staying connected to Him. What are they, exactly?[3]
- Discuss the daily/weekly/annual practices or routines you use to maintain your relationship with God.
- What one thing will you start doing or do more of to get you closer to God?

---

[3] Four benefits of staying connected to Jesus from John 15:7-11 (1). Answered prayers (2) You will produce much fruit (3) Your life will bring glory to God (4) You will be filled with Christ's joy.

2. STOP COMPLAINING AND START BEING GRATEFUL

Philippians 2:14: "Do everything without complaining and arguing" (NLT).

Colossians 2:7: "Let your lives OVERFLOW with thanksgiving for all God has done" (LB).

- Read the two verses above about complaining and gratitude. God seems to value thankfulness over complaining; explain why you think that is the case.
- Why do you think it's better to focus on the good things God has done for you instead of the bad things that have happened to you?

3. STOP COMPARING AND START BEING CONTENT

Proverbs 14:30: "It's healthy to be content, but envy will eat you up" (CEV).

1 Timothy 6:6: "Godliness with contentment is great gain" (NIV).

- Read the two verses above about envy and contentment. Why do you think God prefers an attitude of contentment over comparing (envy)?
- In light of Proverbs 14:30, what do you think envy does to people?
- In what ways can you benefit from adopting an attitude of contentment?

4. STOP BEING TIGHT-FISTED AND START BEING GENEROUS

Haggai 1:6-7,9-10: "You have food to eat, but NOT ENOUGH to make you full. You have wine to drink, but NOT ENOUGH to get drunk on! You have clothing, but NOT ENOUGH to keep you warm. And workers CAN NOT EARN ENOUGH to live on. Can't you see why this has happened? ... Because my Temple lies in ruins while every one of you is busy working on your own house. That is why there is no rain, and NOTHING CAN GROW" (GN).

- What stands out to you in the above Scripture?
- From the above scripture, how come God's people don't have enough to live on?
- Can you discern God's message in this passage of Scripture?

Mike shares, "God hardwires this universal law into the universe: The more you give to others, the more you will receive in return. God's generosity has given us everything, and He calls on us to share what we have with those in need. He promises blessing upon our lives in proportion to the good we do for others."

- What does this teaching mean to you?

Luke 6:38 Jesus says: "If you give, you will get! Your gift will return to you in FULL and OVERFLOWING measure, pressed down, shaken together to make room for more, and RUNNING OVER. Whatever measure you use to give—large or small—will be used to measure what is given back to you" (NLT)

- What phrases or thoughts jump out to you from Luke 6:38?
- According to Luke 6:38, what can a person do to receive a "full and overflowing" blessing?
- What does Jesus' teaching from Luke 6:38 mean to you? How would you apply that to your life?

SECTION 3: PERSONAL COMMITMENT AND APPLICATION

a) Consider adopting these four principles to enjoy the overflowing life. (1) Stay connected to Jesus daily! (2) Stop complaining and start being grateful. (3) Stop comparing and start being content. And (4) Stop being tight-fisted and start being generous

b) What personal application has the Lord shown you from the message? How do you feel about following through with it?

D. PRAYER POINTS

1. Pray that you and the other members of your Small Group will respond positively to this message and will act on it.

2. Pray for a miraculous outcome as you and your group put this wisdom into practice.

3. Ask everyone in the group to share what they need prayer for, and then pray for those requests.

4. Request that one of your members lead in a closing prayer.

PLEASE REACH OUT TO ANYONE WHO DID NOT
MAKE IT TO YOUR MEETING

Chapter 2—Turning Setbacks Into Success

Using This Discussion Guide

This is only a guide. This discussion guide contains too many questions for most groups to answer in a single session. You may choose a few questions from each section after considering the needs of your group.

A. OPEN YOUR SESSION WITH PRAYER

B. INTRODUCTION:

This Bible study looks at Joseph's life to teach that what matters in life is not your circumstances but your character and to demonstrate God's strategy for turning setbacks into successes.

C. BIBLE DISCUSSION: PICK THE POINTS YOU WANT TO DISCUSS.

SECTION 1: PERSONALIZING THE MESSAGE

    a) What do you think was the most eye-opening part of the message? Why?

    b) What part of the message inspired confidence, renewed your faith, or gave you confidence?

    c) What did you read that challenged or convicted you?

    d) How did the message deepen your love for God?

e) What positive result could occur from heeding the message or the painful consequences of disregarding its truth?

SECTION 2: DIGGING DEEPER

Mike notes in the Joseph story that jealous people, like Joseph's brothers, will try to hurt you; immoral people, like Mrs. Potiphar, will try to tempt you; and ambitious people, like the steward from prison, will try to use you.

- How would you react if you were in Joseph's situation?
- How has your suffering impacted your personality, outlook in life, and faith?

Despite his setbacks, Joseph was successful. *"The Lord was with Joseph"* explains Joseph's prosperity. The Bible says:

Genesis 39:2: "THE LORD WAS WITH JOSEPH so that he prospered, and he lived in the house of his Egyptian master" (NIV).

Genesis 39:3: "Joseph's master saw that THE LORD WAS WITH JOSEPH and that the Lord gave him success in everything he did" (NIV).

Genesis 39:20-21: "While Joseph was in prison, THE LORD WAS WITH HIM; He showed him kindness and granted him favor" (NIV).

Genesis 39:23: "THE LORD WAS WITH JOSEPH and gave him success in whatever he did" (NIV).

- What do you notice about the Scripture verses listed above?
- According to the scriptures, what is the key to Joseph's breakthrough and success?
- Mike observes that it makes no difference who or what is opposing you. The presence of God in your

life is a game changer. What does this teaching mean to you?

- Has Christ solved a problem you could not have solved on your own? If so, how did you achieve your breakthrough?
- Do you believe Jesus can solve your problem today? Why or why not?

THREE CHARACTER TRAITS FROM JOSEPH'S LIFE TO TURN SETBACKS INTO SUCCESS

I MUST FULFILL MY RESPONSIBILITIES

Genesis 39:6: "Potiphar gave Joseph COMPLETE RESPONSIBILITY over everything he owned. With Joseph there, he didn't worry about a thing" (NLT).

Genesis 39:22-23: "The jailer soon handed over the entire prison administration to Joseph . . . and had no more worries after that, for Joseph took care of everything" (LB).

- According to Genesis 39:6 and 39:22-23, why do you think Potiphar (Joseph's boss) and the jailer handed over responsibility to Joseph?
- What does this message teach you about what decision-makers look for when considering someone for promotion?

Mike observes that your strong work ethic will propel you forward. "Hard work pays off" is more than a cliche; it is also true in the workplace. Hard work is required for high performance. Employers look for employees with a strong work ethic to hire and promote. Hard work yields career advancement and job satisfaction.

- What are your thoughts on this statement?

- If you have experienced career progression, briefly describe your work ethic and how it resulted in your promotion.

Genesis 41:38,40: "Pharaoh said, 'We will never find a better man than Joseph, who has God's Spirit in him. I will put you in charge of my country, and all my people will obey your orders. Your authority will be second only to mine'" (GN)

Mike observes from the above scripture that your work's quality reveals your spiritual life's quality. The Holy Spirit was prominent in Joseph's life. There's a direct correlation between the quality of your work, your Christian witness, and your success.

- What are your thoughts on Genesis 41:38,40 and Mike's remarks above?
- What key factor contributed to Joseph's success?
- Why is it important for Christians to demonstrate our Christian ethics in the workplace, and everywhere we go?

Read the following scripture verses.

"Whatever your hand finds to do, do it WITH ALL YOUR MIGHT" (Ecclesiastes 9:10 NIV).

"Never be lazy in your work, but serve the Lord ENTHUSIASTICALLY" (Romans 12:11 NLT).

"Servants, do what you are told by your earthly masters. And DON'T JUST DO THE MINIMUM that will get you by. DO YOUR BEST!" (Colossians 3:23 MSG).

"Do you see any truly competent workers? They will serve kings rather than working for ordinary people" (Proverbs 22:29 NLT).

Colossians 3:23-24: "Work hard and cheerfully at ALL you do, just as though you were working for the Lord and not merely for your masters. Remember that it is the Lord Christ who is going to pay you. He is the one you are really working for" (LB).

- What do you believe is the central message of the above Scriptures?
- What encourages you about Colossians 3:23-24?
- What do you think will happen if you consistently follow these teachings over time?

Mike notes from Colossians 3:23-24 that every task is an opportunity to develop and demonstrate faithfulness, no matter what. In everything you do, God is watching to reward you according to the quality of your work.

- Briefly share when you or someone's hard work was rewarded or encountered a job loss due to poor performance.

2. I MUST MAINTAIN MY INTEGRITY

Genesis 39:10: "She [Potiphar's wife] kept putting pressure on Joseph day after day, but he refused to sleep with her, and he kept out of her way as much as possible" (NLT).

- Imagine and share the internal battle going on in Joseph's mind.
- How did he avoid Mrs. Potiphar's pressure campaign?
- What do you think would have been the potential consequences if Joseph as a slave, had given in to Mrs. Potiphar's sexual advances?
- What do you think motivated Joseph not to give in?

- How would you react if you were in a similar situation, or what advice would you give to someone who came to you with the same issue? Why?
- Why is it beneficial to always do the right thing?

Genesis 39:8-9: "Joseph refused. "Look," he told her, "MY MASTER TRUSTS ME with everything in his entire household ... How could I do such a wicked thing as this? It would be a great SIN AGAINST GOD!" (NLT).

Mike notes that Joseph evades temptation by upholding his loyalty to his boss and accountability before God. We hurt ourselves when we lower our integrity and do something wrong.

- Share how loyalty to someone and accountability before God are powerful weapons against temptation.

Mike shares, " I encourage you to stay pure. You will save yourself so many heartaches and have God's blessings on your life. There are many stories of those who have been taken down by their flaws, leaders who had everything going well for them but had gotten complacent in their power and self-interest and fallen disgracefully. When you lower any area of integrity, it damages you.

- What thoughts do you have about this teaching?
- How is integrity essential to your success?

3. I MUST TRUST GOD'S SOVEREIGNTY

Mike describes two vital life lessons to help you endure hardships with confidence. (1) Pain often has a hidden purpose. Usually, you don't figure out the purpose until after the pain is over. We rarely see the purpose of it while we're in pain. Also, (2) God often redirects our lives through a failure, mistake, disappointment, broken dream, or crisis. He often re-channels our life the way He wants them to be.

- What does this teaching mean to you?
- Briefly share how God redirected your life from a failure, mistake, or crisis to a better outcome.

Several years later, Joseph's brothers came to Egypt to buy food. They didn't know that their brother, whom they tried to murder and then sold into slavery, was the vice president and in charge of trade and exports. Joseph told them, *"God sent me ahead of you to rescue you in this amazing way to make sure that you and your descendants survive. So, it was not really you who sent me here, but God"* (Genesis 45:7-8 GN).

- Mike points out that the sovereignty of God means as ruler of the universe, God is free and has the right to do whatever He wants. He is not bound or limited by the dictates of His created beings. God's will is the final cause of all things. According to Genesis 45:7-8, how does understanding God's sovereignty at work in your life help you see your difficulties from God's perspective?
- How does accepting and trusting God's sovereignty help you endure the difficult seasons of your life?

Joseph said this to his brothers who tried to murder him:

Genesis 50:20: "Even though you planned evil against me, God planned good to come out of it. This was to keep many people alive, as he is doing now" (GW).

- Perhaps you may have been harmed by someone because of their ill-treatment. How does remembering God's plan to turn it around for your good from Genesis 50:20 help you view yourself as a victim rather than a victim?

- From experience, share a difficult situation that God turned around for good in your life.

Mike shares this scripture to direct our focus on God when it seems like circumstances have disrupted the dream God has for us:

"Trust in the Lord with all your heart and lean not on your own understanding. In all your ways, submit to Him, and He will make your paths straight" (Proverbs 3:5-6 NIV).

- From Proverbs 3:5-6, what three actions should you take for God to make things right for you?
- Life struggles disrupt our peace and joy and cause insecurities (worry, fear, doubt, etc.). Why do you think the actions from Proverbs 3:5-6 can restore your emotional health?

Mike shares that when going through a circumstance he doesn't like, he asks himself three questions to align with God's ways: (1) Is it my fault? A lot of things I bring on myself. (2) What can I learn from this? (3) How does God want me to do in this circumstance?

- What are your thoughts on this statement?
- How does trusting God's sovereignty helpful in your recovery from setbacks?

SECTION 3: PERSONAL COMMITMENT AND APPLICATION

a) Consider adopting these three principles to enjoy recovery and success. (1) Fulfill your responsibilities, (2) Maintain your integrity, and (3) Trust God's sovereignty.

b) What personal application has the Lord shown you from the message? How do you feel about following through with it?

D. PRAYER POINTS

1. Pray that you and the other members of your Small Group will respond positively to this message and will act on it.
2. Pray for a miraculous outcome as you and your group put this wisdom into practice.
3. Ask everyone in the group to share what they need prayer for, and then pray for those requests.
4. Request that one of your members lead in a closing prayer.

PLEASE REACH OUT TO ANYONE WHO DID NOT
MAKE IT TO YOUR MEETING

Chapter 3—How to See Your Dreams Become a Reality

"The Lord holds success in store for the upright" (Proverbs 2:7 NIV)

Using This Discussion Guide

This is only a guide. This discussion guide contains too many questions for most groups to answer in a single session. You may choose a few questions from each section after considering the needs of your group.

A. OPEN YOUR SESSION WITH PRAYER

B. INTRODUCTION:

This Bible discussion explores the practical steps to accomplish your dreams, vision, and goals from the classic chapter of success in the Bible — Genesis Chapter 24. The word "success" is used five times in this Bible passage concerning Abraham's servant's quest to find a wife for Isaac.

C. BIBLE DISCUSSION: PICK THE POINTS YOU WANT TO DISCUSS

SECTION 1: PERSONALIZING THE MESSAGE

a) What insights from the message left the biggest impression on you? Why?

b) What encouraged or reassured you from the message?

c) What did you read that challenged or convicted you?

d) How did the message increase your appreciation for God the Father, Jesus Christ, or the Holy Spirit?

e) What positive result could occur from heeding the message or the painful consequences of disregarding its truth?

SECTION 2: DIGGING DEEPER

Mike opens this chapter with quotes from four successful individuals — Tim Cook, Bill Gates, Venus Williams, and Alexander Bell—on the value of a focused life.

- What are your thoughts on these quotes from the chapter?

STEP ONE: YOU MUST DETERMINE YOUR CURRENT POSITION

Mike shares, "You can't figure out where you want to go until you know where you already are. To determine your present position, you should ask yourself two questions: *'Where am I now?'* and, *'what would I like to change?'*"

- Please take a moment to ponder over these questions and answer them.

Mike suggests that whatever you intend to do with your life, you'd better get on it for two reasons: Number one, everything meaningful takes longer than you think. And number two, you are not getting any younger. So, whatever you want to do with your life, you must do it now.

- What are your thoughts on this statement?

STEP TWO: YOU MUST DECIDE EXACTLY WHAT YOU WANT

Abraham paints a clear picture for his servant Eliezer. He tells him what he wants and what he doesn't want. *"Don't get a wife for my son from the Canaanite girls who live around here. Instead, go back to my country, to the land of my relatives, and get a wife for my son Isaac"* (Genesis 24:3-4 NCV).

- Based on Genesis 24:3-4, what are Abraham's specific instructions to his servant?
- What is the importance of being specific with your life goals?

Mike suggests you ask yourself four questions to help you qualify your life goals: (1) What do I want to be in the next five or ten years? (2) What do I want to do? (3) What do I want to have? (4) Why do I want it?

- Please take a moment to consider these questions and answer them.
- In what way does this exercise helpful in formulating your life goals?

Eliezer, Abraham's servant, gets worried and anxious. "Then the servant asked Abraham, ' *WHAT IF the woman [whom he's going to find] is unwilling to leave her home [in Iraq] and come back with me [a stranger] to this land"* [to marry a guy she's never met]? (Genesis 24:5 NIV, emphasis added, parenthesis mine).

- Why do you think Abraham's servant asked the question?
- Mike shares, "When God gives you a dream, dwelling on the worse case scenarios could keep you from fulfilling your destiny because there will be a long laundry list of them, and you'll never get around to

starting. Worry and fear will cause you to procrastinate and, eventually, force you to abandon your dream."

- What thoughts do you have on this teaching?
- What could happen when you believe your doubts or what naysayers say instead of trusting God?

STEP THREE: YOU NEED A PROMISE FROM GOD

Mike shares, at this stage, "Focus on God's provision, not your problems. Focus on what God has promised to do, not what you don't have in your life. The Bible is loaded with promises of security, safety, provision, prosperity, success, stability, strength, wisdom, and much more. They're just blank checks waiting for you to claim."

- What are the advantages of believing in God's promises?
- Share a promise from God's Word that has been encouraging to you. Why?

Abraham relieved Eliezer's "what if" fears with this statement: "The LORD, the God of heaven, brought me from the home of my father and the land of my relatives. And HE PROMISED ME, *'I will give this land to your DESCENDANTS.'* *The LORD will send His angel before you to help you get a wife for my son there"* (Genesis 24:7 NCV).

- After reading Genesis 24:7, what words or ideas jump out to you? What do you think the main message is?
- From Genesis 24:7, why do you think Abraham felt so strongly about sending his servant to his homeland?
- What can Abraham's servant trust in as he goes on this challenging mission?

- How does this Scripture verse answer any doubts and worries about God's promises concerning your life?

STEP FOUR: ASK GOD FOR HELP

Genesis 24:12: *"Eliezer prayed, 'O Lord, God of my master Abraham. Give me success and show this kindness to my master, Abraham. Help me to accomplish the purpose of my journey"* (NLT 1996).

- In Genesis 24:12, what specifically does Abraham's servant pray for?
- Why is it beneficial to approach God with specific requests instead of vague prayers?

Mike shares, "Abraham's servant avoided many potential missteps. He could have failed in the mission. The "sign" at the well could have been missed. Laban could have refused to give his daughter's hand in marriage to a stranger, or Rebekah could have been unwilling to come along with him. But God worked out everything behind the scenes. When you pray, you can trust God's guidance because He is gracious and will never leave His people to fend for themselves. He is a prayer-answering God!"

- How does this teaching encourage you to pray for God's help?
- When is it okay to pray for success in our efforts?
- Why is it beneficial to approach God with specific requests instead of vague prayers?
- Briefly share a situation where God worked things out behind the scenes to bring you victory.

"Let us then approach God's throne of grace with confidence, so that we may receive mercy and find grace to help us in our time of need" (Hebrews 4:16 NIV).

- According to Hebrews 4:16, how should you pray, and what are the expected results?
- In your opinion, what are some ways you could confidently approach the throne of God?
- Why are we often hesitant to approach God in confidence?

STEP FIVE: IDENTIFY THE ROADBLOCKS

In this step, Mike suggests you list the roadblocks to achieving your goal—financially, educationally, emotionally, relationally, or whatever—and look at them honestly. It means asking yourself the following discovery questions to uncover potential roadblocks or obstacles: Why don't I have what I want? Or Why am I not who I want to be? Or Why don't I do what I want to do?

- Take a moment to reflect on the discovery questions and share your response.

STEP SIX: CREATE AN ACTION PLAN

Mike shares, "To reach your goal and fulfill your destiny, you need to create a step-by-step action plan. You take it one step at a time. You don't try to do it all at once; instead, you spread it out. Eliezer designed a simple yet well-thought-off plan to find the right woman for Isaac."

- Why is it beneficial to create a step-by-step plan to get you where you want to be?
- What do you think might happen if you fail to plan?

Mike describes, "A plan has at least three parts: *action steps, a schedule, and a deadline.* So, you want to ask yourself three questions as you make a plan. (1) What action steps must I take to move the dream along. (2) What is the schedule of activities or action steps I need to take? And (3) When do I intend to get to the end stage—deadline (in 2, 3, 5, or 10 years)?

- What are your thoughts on this statement?
- What other steps might you include in a step-by-step plan to get you where you want to be?

STEP SEVEN: BE PATIENT AND PERSISTENT

Mike shares, "Nothing great is ever accomplished without an extra dose of patience, persistence, determination, and endurance. So, it would be best if you were patient and persistent because it doesn't happen overnight. It takes time and energy to accomplish significant goals.

- What are your thoughts on this statement?
- Briefly share how patience and persistence have impacted your life journey.

Habakkuk 2:3: *"These things I plan won't happen right away. Slowly, steadily, surely, the time approaches when the vision will be fulfilled. If it seems slow, do not despair, for these things will surely come to pass. Just be patient! They will not be overdue a single day!"* (LB).

- What words or ideas jump out to you from Habakkuk 2:3?
- What does this Scripture passage teach you??
- According to Habakkuk 2:3, how will the things that God has planned happen?
- How do you feel about the eventual certainty that God's promise will be fulfilled for you?
- God is more interested in what you are becoming than what you are doing. What does this verse suggest you should do when planned things do not happen right away?

According to Genesis 24:21, Abraham's servant watched Rebekah closely until she drew water for all his camels to learn whether the Lord had made his journey successful. Similarly, in Genesis 24:33, Abraham's servant would not even eat until he told Rebekah and her family the purpose of his journey and heard their response.

- What do these passages teach you about patience and persistence in getting where you want to be?

STEP EIGHT: YOU MUST ENLIST A TEAM FOR SUPPORT

Mike shares, "You are never going to fulfill your vision yourself. This is important because your major successes are never a one-person show. You must involve other people. It takes teamwork and cooperation."

- What are your thoughts on this statement?

Ecclesiastes 4:12: *"A person standing alone can be attacked and defeated, but two can stand back-to-back and conquer. Three are even better, for a triple-braided cord is not easily broken"* (NLT).

- What is the advantage of standing alongside other people, according to Ecclesiastes 4:12?
- How might you apply this passage to your life?
- An African proverb says, "If you want to go fast, go by yourself, but if you want to go far, go with others." Why might you be able to accomplish far more together than by yourself?

STEP NINE: YOU MUST PAY THE PRICE

Eliezer had to pay a price to get Rebekah to go back with him. *"Then the servant brought out gold and silver jewelry and articles of clothing and gave them to Rebekah; he also gave costly gifts to her brother and mother"* (Genesis 24:53 NIV).

- From Genesis 24:53, in what ways did Abraham's servant bless Rebekah and her family?
- Why are people sometimes reluctant to pay the price to get where they want to be?
- What sacrifice are you willing to pay to get God's best in your life?

Mike shares, Great goals always require great sacrifice. In setting your goals, ask the following questions: (1) What will it cost me? (2) What am I willing to give up? (3) Is the goal or the cause worth it?

- What are your thoughts on this teaching? Take a moment and reflect on your questions.

SECTION 3: PERSONAL APPLICATION AND COMMITMENT

Developing a focused life that leads to major success is not a short-term project. It requires work, dedication, patience, and persistence. It also requires you to depend upon God and obey Him. You need God's help and direction at every step in the process. Never confuse the decision-making process with the problem-solving phase. Once you figure out the "what" and "why," God will show you the "how." He has given over 7,000 promises in the Bible. You need to attach one or more of these promises to your development goals. This will encourage you to pursue your goals and inspire you to focus on God's promises and not on the problems.

- Are you willing to commit to creating a focused life?
- Start now by asking God for direction and to bring people into your life to support your effort.

- Become familiar with the promises of God that relate to the goals you want to develop.
- Commit to following and refining these steps as the Lord directs.

D. PRAYER POINTS

1. Pray that you and the other members of your Small Group will respond positively to this message and will act on it.
2. Pray for a miraculous outcome as you and your group put this wisdom into practice.
3. Ask everyone in the group to share what they need prayer for, and then pray for those requests.
4. Request that one of your members lead in a closing prayer.

PLEASE REACH OUT TO ANYONE WHO DID NOT
MAKE IT TO YOUR MEETING

Chapter 4—How to Overcome the Enemy Within

"Don't fear anything except the Lord! If you fear Him, you need fear nothing else" (Isaiah 8:13 LB)

Using This Discussion Guide

This is only a guide. This discussion guide contains too many questions for most groups to answer in a single session. You may choose a few questions from each section after considering the needs of your group.

A. OPEN YOUR SESSION WITH PRAYER

B. INTRODUCTION:

This Bible study discussion will cover the five major fears that keep us from fulfilling our destiny. They are incompetence, embarrassment, rejection, comparison & failure, and commitment. Moses' reaction when God told him to go to Egypt to free the Israelites exemplifies these fears. God responded to each of Moses' concerns. If we learn how God responded to Moses' fears, we can apply that response when we are afraid to do what God has called us to do.

C. BIBLE DISCUSSION: PICK THE POINTS YOU WANT TO DISCUSS.

SECTION 1: PERSONALIZING THE MESSAGE

a) Which part(s) of the message stood out most to you? Why?
b) What part of the message inspired confidence, renewed your faith, or gave you confidence?
c) What did you read that challenged or convicted you?
d) How did the message deepen your love for God?
e) What positive result could occur from heeding the message or the painful consequences of disregarding its truth?

SECTION 2: DIGGING DEEPER

Mike cites Max Lucado: "Fear. His modus operandi is to manipulate you with the mysterious, to taunt you with the unknown. Fear of death, fear of failure, fear of God, fear of tomorrow—his arsenal is vast. His goal? To create cowardly, joyless souls. He doesn't want you to make the journey to the mountain. He figures if he can rattle you enough, you will take your eyes off the peaks and settle for a dull existence in the flatlands."

• What are your thoughts on this statement?
• From your personal experience, how has fear affected you or someone you know?

1. THE FEAR OF INCOMPETENCE

Exodus 3:11: "But Moses said to God, 'Who am I, that I should go to Pharaoh and bring the Israelites out of Egypt?'" (NIV).

29

- From Exodus 3:11, what did Moses say when God told him to bring the Israelites out of Egypt?
- Why is it that when God calls on us, our first reaction, like Moses, is often: "Who, me?"
- What does it say about our level of faith if we question God when He chooses us for a task?

God says: *"I will be with you"* Exodus 3:12 (NIV).

- In Exodus 3:12, what response did God give to Moses?
- Why should it make a difference that God has promised to be with you?
- How does God's presence solve your fear of incompetence?

1 Peter 2:9: *"You have been chosen by God Himself … you are God's very own"* (LB)

- From 1 Peter 2:9, what words or ideas jump out to you? What does this Scripture mean to you? What do you think the main message is?
- How does it make you feel knowing that God has chosen you despite your circumstances?

2. THE FEAR OF EMBARRASSMENT

Exodus 3:13: "But Moses protested, "If I go to the people of Israel and tell them, 'The God of your ancestors has sent me to you,' they won't believe me. They will ask, 'Which God are you talking about? What is his name?' Then what should I tell them? (NLT96).

- From Exodus 3:13, what does Moses fear the Israelites' response will be? What is Moses' question to God?

- Why do people feel embarrassed when they don't know the answers?
- Although this was another excuse from Moses, at least he asked a good question: "Which God are you talking about?" Why is it essential that every Christian be able to answer this question?

Exodus 3:14-15: "God said to Moses, "I am who I am! This is what you are to say to the Israelites: 'I AM has sent me to you ... This is My name forever, the name by which I am to be remembered from generation to generation" (NIV)

- What was God's response in Exodus 3:14–15?
- In the Old Testament, a person's name expresses their character. God says, "I am who I am! This My name forever." God's name tells us four things: God exists; God is eternal; God is truth; God doesn't change. How does God say He is to be remembered by us? How well are you living up to this command?

Mike points out, "The only foundation for a fearless life is building your life on something that never changes. God is the only thing in life that doesn't change. The world changes, you change, and your relationships change. If you build your life on anything except God, you'll constantly fear the next change. Only God is unchanging.

- What does this teaching mean to you?
- In what ways can you come to know God more personally?
- How can knowing God erase your fears?

3. FEAR OF REJECTION

Exodus 4:1: "But Moses said, "They won't believe me! They won't do what I tell them to. They'll say, 'Jehovah never appeared to you!' (LB).

- In Exodus 4:1, what does Moses assume the Israelites will think and say to him?
- The fear of rejection is universal. How might you react to people if you were in Moses' shoes?
- What is the difference between rejection by people versus rejection by God?

Proverbs 29:25: *"Fear of man is a dangerous trap, but to trust in God means safety"* (LB).

- From Proverbs 29:25, why do you think fearing people is a dangerous trap, but trusting God means safety?

Exodus 4:2–4: *"2 The Lord asked Moses, "What is that in your hand?" "A shepherd's staff," Moses replied. 3 "Throw it down on the ground," the Lord told him. So Moses threw down the staff, and it turned into a snake! 4 Then the Lord told him, "Reach out and grab its tail." So Moses reached out and grabbed it, and it turned back into a shepherd's staff in his hand"* (NLT).

- What did God ask Moses, and what was his response in Exodus 4:2?

Mike shares that in biblical days, a shepherd's staff represents a person's identity, influence, and income. After this incident, Moses' staff was known as "The Rod of God." When Moses laid the rod down, God's power was in effect. When Moses picked it up, it was simply dead wood. God can work wonders in our lives if we allow and follow him.

- What impression do you have about Moses' staff becoming "The Rod of God" when he obeyed God?
- Based on Exodus 4:2-4 and the teaching, what can happen when we don't let go—or won't go when God desires us to?

Mike states, "When you let God control every bit of your life, you're not afraid of rejection and someone disapproving of you because you know God is on your side and is using you."

- How can surrendering to God erase your fears?

4. THE FEAR OF COMPARISON AND FAILURE

Mike shares, "The fear of comparison is when you start looking around and comparing yourself to what other people are doing and then feeling inadequate. This leads to the fear of failure that could stop you from taking steps to move forward to achieve your goals."

- From your experience, how has a fear of comparison and failure affected you or someone you know?

Mike explains, "Past failures, if not dealt with, may make people afraid of failing everywhere. Perfectionists tend to have this fear. For them, it is all about doing everything perfectly. Anything less than perfection seems like a dismal and humiliating failure that can't be tolerated.

This fear of comparison and failure can stop people from trying altogether, no matter how golden the opportunity looks.

- Why do you think dwelling on past failures or perfectionism can stop you from living your God-ordained destiny?

  Exodus 4:10: "But Moses pleaded with the Lord, "O Lord, I'm not very good with words. I have never been, and I'm not now, even though you have spoken to me. I get tongue-tied, and my words get tangled" (NLT).

  - According to Exodus 4:10, how did Moses respond to God's command?
  - How can we know our abilities and capacity to serve God without attempting what He calls us to do first?

- Why do we compare our talent and abilities to others instead of obeying God's command?

Exodus 4:11–12: "Then the Lord asked Moses. 'Who makes mouths? *Who makes people so they can speak or not speak, hear or not hear, see or not see? Is it not I, the Lord? Now go and do as I have told you. I will help you speak well, and I will tell you what to say"* (NLT96).

- What were God's responses to Moses, according to Exodus 4:11-12?
- Why do you think God refocused Moses on Him?
- Why is it common to trust ourselves and others instead of trying God? How can this choice rob us of blessings?
- Like Moses, God often calls people to do what they cannot do alone. Why is that? Is there any way God is calling you to serve that is more challenging than you can by yourself?

Matthew 10:19–20: Jesus: *"Don't worry about what you'll say or how you'll say it. The right words will be there; the Spirit of your Father will supply the words"* (MSG)

2 Timothy 2:17: *"God has not given us a spirit of fear and timidity, but of power, love, and self-discipline"* (NLT).

- According to Matthew 10:19-20 and 2 Timothy 2:17, what resources has God promised to give us to overcome worry and fear?
- Mike shares, "God's answer for fear of comparison and failure is relying on Him!" Why is reliance on God a fear-reliever?

5. THE FEAR OF COMMITMENT

Exodus 4:13: *"But Moses answered, "No, Lord, please send someone else"* (GN).

- From Exodus 4:13, what was Moses' final plea to God?
- Mike explained that Moses did not care. He was comfortable and didn't want to take a risk of this magnitude. What are some of the comforts or obstacles—real or imagined—which could keep people from serving God?
- We often feel we cannot do what God calls us to accomplish. What are some ways to go forward even when fear threatens to stop you?

Exodus 4:14: "Then the Lord became angry with Moses" (NLT).

- What was God's response to Moses in Exodus 4:14 after all his objections were addressed?
- Why was God angry with Moses?
- What is God telling you to do that requires trusting Him?
- From Exodus 4:13&14, Moses forgot to put God first. What are some of the "buts" keeping you from trusting God and placing Him first?

SECTION 3: PERSONAL APPLICATION AND COMMITMENT

God's presence is the cure for fear of incompetence. His eternal character is His cure for embarrassment. Surrendering to God's will is the antidote to rejection fear. His solution to the fear of comparison and fear is to rely on Him! Submission to God's will is God's remedy for fear of commitment. This week, ask God to help you identify the fears that keep you from doing what He wants you to do. Pray to God to help you overcome your fears and do His will.

E. PRAYER POINTS

1. Pray that you and the other members of your Small Group will respond positively to this message and will act on it.
2. Pray for a miraculous outcome as you and your group put this wisdom into practice.
3. Ask everyone in the group to share what they need prayer for, and then pray for those requests.
4. Request that one of your members lead in a closing prayer.

PLEASE REACH OUT TO ANYONE WHO DID NOT MAKE IT TO YOUR MEETING

Chapter 5—How to Be Confident and Victorious in Crisis

"The Lord will be our Mighty One. He will be like a wide river of protection that no enemy can cross, that no enemy ship can sail upon"
(Isaiah 33:21 NLT)

Using This Discussion Guide

This is only a guide. This discussion guide contains too many questions for most groups to answer in a single session. You may choose a few questions from each section after considering the needs of your group.

A. OPEN YOUR SESSION WITH PRAYER

B. INTRODUCTION:

This Bible discussion explores why we experience "storms" (hardships) in life, how "storms" affect us, and how we can be confident and overcome them based on the story of Paul and his fellow sailors' shipwreck from Acts 27.

C. BIBLE DISCUSSION: PICK THE POINTS YOU WANT TO DISCUSS.

SECTION 1: PERSONALIZING THE MESSAGE

a) What insights from the message left the biggest impression on you? Why?

b) What encouraged or reassured you from the message?

c) What did you read that challenged or convicted you?

d) How did the message increase your appreciation for God the Father, Jesus Christ, or the Holy Spirit?

e) What positive result could occur from heeding the message or the painful consequences of disregarding its truth?

SECTION 2: DIGGING DEEPER

WHY WE EXPERIENCE "STORMS" IN LIFE

WE LISTEN TO THE WRONG EXPERTS

Acts 27:11 says, *"The centurion, instead of listening to what Paul said, followed the advice of the pilot and of the owner of the ship" (NIV).*

- Why do you think the centurion listened to the pilot and the ship owner and dismissed Paul's advice?

- Why do you think people choose to follow the wrong leaders?

Mike shares that so many quack "practitioners" on social media tell you what to do. If you follow most of them, you will ruin your marriage, finances, job, health, spiritual walk, and life."

- What are your thoughts on this statement?

- What should you do if you are given an important opinion about your life?

2. WE ACT INSTINCTIVELY ON POPULAR OPINION

Acts 27:12 says, *"Since the harbor was unsuitable in winter, THE MAJORITY DECIDED that we should sail on, hoping to reach Phoenix and winter there. This was a harbor in Crete that was facing both southwest and northwest" (NIV).*

- What factors resulted in the decision to sail?

- Should you always follow the majority or popular opinion? Why or why not?

Exodus 23:2 says, *"Do not follow the majority when they do wrong or when they give testimony that perverts justice"* (GN).

- What does Exodus 23:2 mean to you, and how would you apply its message?
- Why is it risky to act on popular opinion or do the most popular thing without verifying its accuracy?

Mike cites Socrates, *"We must not regard what the many say of us; but what He, the One man who has an understanding of just and unjust, will say, and what the truth will say."*

- Whom does Socrates refer to as the "One man who understands the just and unjust."
- Why should we prioritize God's viewpoints over the majority's?

3. WE IMPULSIVELY RELY ON CIRCUMSTANCES

Paul cautions, *"I can see that our voyage is going to be disastrous and bring great loss to ship and cargo, and to our own lives also"* (Acts 27:10 NIV).

- What is the message of Paul's vision from Acts 27:10?
- What should we do when we receive a clear message from God? Why?

Acts 27:13 says, *"When a GENTLE south wind began to blow, they saw their opportunity; so they weighed anchor and sailed along the shore of Crete"* (NIV).

- According to Acts 27:13, what were the circumstances the sailors saw as their opportunity to sail contrary to Paul's divine vision?
- Why is it unwise to ignore what God says, even when circumstances contradict it?

HOW "STORMS" TEND TO AFFECT OUR LIVES

The Bible says, *"The ship was caught by the storm and could not head into the wind, so we gave way to it and were driven along. [We] lowered the anchor and let the ship be driven along"* Acts 27: 15, 17b NIV). Mike describes, "Sometimes life seems like that. You get a problem, and the strong currents of life sweep you back and forth. You don't know where you're going. You lose sight of your goal and want to say, "What's the use? Why fight it? I'll just go with the flow."

- What is your experience with the above Bible verse and Mike's description of how life's "storm" affects us?

"We took such a violent battering from the storm that they began throwing the cargo overboard. They threw the ship's tackle overboard. They lightened the ship further by throwing all the wheat overboard. They ordered everyone who could swim to jump overboard first and swim ashore; the rest were to follow, holding on to the planks or some broken pieces of the ship" (Acts 27:18-19, 38, 43-44 NIV+GW).

- What items did the sailors throw overboard?
- What do you think is going on, based on your imagination?

Mike explains, "Often, when we get in a crisis, we are tempted to throw out the things that are important to us or the values we've held onto in better times. We become impulsive and look for items to discard in our lives. We give up on our dreams and throw away our Christian priorities."

- What are your thoughts on Mike's description of a crisis reaction?
- What are some of the valuables people discard or unfavorable decisions they make when under pressure?

Acts 27:20 says, *"For a number of days, we couldn't see the sun or the stars. The storm wouldn't let up. It was so severe that we finally began to lose any hope of coming out of it alive"* (GW). Mike describes, "The last thing you throw out when you've got a problem is hope. When you throw that away, you've had it."

- Using your imagination, what do you think is happening in Acts 27:20?
- Why is hope valuable in life, particularly in times of crisis?

Mike suggests, "The sailors had forgotten that God was in control even in the midst of their storm. They had forgotten that God had a plan and that He could inject hope into a desperately hopeless situation."

- Share a time when God brought hope into a difficult situation. How was that beneficial to you?

Psalm 125:1 says, *"Those who trust in the Lord are steady as Mount Zion, unmoved by any circumstance"* (LB).

- From Psalm 125:1, what words or ideas jump out to you?
- What do you think the main message is?
- How do we receive this promise?

- How do you think this promise will promote strength, confidence, and hope in times of crisis if you hold on to it?

ANCHORS TO HOLD ONTO IN A "STORM"

1. "STORMS" CAN NOT HIDE THE FACE OF GOD. THEREFORE, I MUST HOLD ON TO *GOD'S PRESENCE.*

Paul said: *"Now I advise you to have courage. No one will lose his life. Only the ship will be destroyed. I know this because an angel from the God to whom I belong and serve stood by me last night"* (Acts 27:22-23 GW).

- In Acts 27:22-23, what assurances did Paul give the worried sailors?
- Why did Paul have that kind of confidence?

Mike shares, "The first anchor in a crisis is the presence of God. You may think God is a million miles away, but He is closer to you than you think. He sees you and is with you. God sent an angel to remind and assure Paul, "I'm with you!" God makes the same commitment to you in the Bible: *Hebrews 13:5 says, "God has said, 'Never will I leave you; never will I forsake you'"* (NIV).

- From Hebrews 13:5, what kind of help does God provide you in troubled times?
- Share a time when you were aware of God's presence. How did that affect your strength, confidence, joy, or peace? OR
- If you have not experienced the ever-present God, has a loved one been by your side during a difficult time? How did that strengthen or encourage you? Imagine the more outstanding experience if the all-loving, all-powerful God was by your side during a difficulty?

Psalm 46:1-3,7: *"God is our protection and our strength. He always helps in times of trouble. So we will not be afraid even if the earth shakes, the mountains fall into the sea, the oceans roar and foam, or the mountains shake at the raging sea. The Lord All-Powerful is with us; the God of Jacob is our defender"* (GW).

- How does Psalm 46:1-3, 7 encourage you to be calm and confident in crisis?
- Briefly share an experience where God protected you in a discouraging or dangerous situation.

Isaiah 43:2-3 says, *"When you pass through deep waters, I will be with you; your troubles will not overwhelm you. When you pass through the fire, you will not be burned; the hard trials that come will not hurt you. For I am the Lord your God"* (GN).

- From Isaiah 43:2-3, what words or ideas jump out to you?
- What does God's message in Isaiah 43:2-3 mean to you?
- Which of the promises made in Isaiah 43:2-3 do you need most today? Why would it bring comfort, peace, and hope to you?

2. "STORMS" CAN NOT CHANGE THE *PURPOSE OF GOD* FOR MY LIFE. MY DESTINY IS SECURE IN GOD

Paul says, *"This angel stood beside me ... and said, `Do not be afraid, Paul. You MUST stand trial before Caesar, and God has graciously given you the lives of all those who sail with you"* (Acts 27:23-24 NIV).

- From Acts 27:23-24, what was God's purpose for Paul?

Mike describes, "God's purpose for Paul was to stand before Caesar, and while he had some skirmishes, he ended up in Rome and fulfilled God's greater purpose for his life—writing the Bible books of Philippians, Colossians, Philemon, and Ephesians. As a Christian, you must have a sense of destiny. God absolutely has a unique purpose and a plan for your life."

- In what ways has God worked out His plans for your life despite your difficulties?

Jeremiah 29:11 says, *"I know the plans I have for you,"* declares the Lord, *"plans to prosper you and not to harm you, plans to give you hope and a future"* (NIV).

- What words or ideas from Jeremiah 29:11 stand out to you?
- What do you think the main message is?
- From Jeremiah 29:11, what are God's purposes for your life?
- How can this Scripture be a source of comfort to you in difficult times?

Romans 11:29 says, *"God's gifts and His call can never be withdrawn; He will never go back on His promises"* (LB).

- What does this promise mean to you?
- How does it encourage you to lean on God during challenging times?

3. "STORMS" CAN NOT DESTROY THE CHILD OF GOD. I MUST RELY ON GOD'S PROMISES

Paul assured the sailors, *"God told me we're going to survive the storm"* (Acts 7:23-24). Paul adds: *"So keep up your courage, men, for I have faith in God that it will happen just as He told me"* (Acts 27:25 NIV).

- What would this message mean to you if you were one of the scared, discouraged sailors? How would you feel?
- Does God keep His promises? How has God kept any of His promises for you?

Jesus: *"Have FAITH in God. I tell you the truth, you can say to this mountain, 'May you be lifted up and thrown into the sea,' and it will happen. But you must REALLY BELIEVE IT WILL HAPPEN and HAVE NO DOUBT in your heart"* (Mark 11:22-23 NLT).

- What three things does Jesus say we should do to have our mountains (problems) removed?
- Based on Mark 11:22-23, explain the relationship between faith and believe.

"When daylight came, they saw a bay with a sandy beach, where they decided to run the ship aground if they could. The ship struck a sandbar and ran aground. They ordered those who could swim to jump overboard first and get to land. The rest were to get there on planks or other pieces of the ship. In this way, everyone reached land safely" (Acts 27:39,41,43-44 NIV).

Mike shares, "That's a happy ending. All 276 sailors made it to shore safely because God gave them a promise and kept it!"

- What does this passage say to you? How would you apply this to your life?

SECTION 3: PERSONAL APPLICATION AND COMMITMENT

a) What personal application has the Lord shown you from the message?
b) How do you feel about following through with it?

D. PRAYER POINTS

1. Pray that you and the other members of your Small Group will respond positively to this message and will act on it.
2. Pray for a miraculous outcome as you and your group put this wisdom into practice.
3. Ask everyone in the group to share what they need prayer for, and then pray for those requests.
4. Request that one of your members lead in a closing prayer.

PLEASE REACH OUT TO ANYONE WHO DID NOT
MAKE IT TO YOUR MEETING

Chapter 6—How to Break Free From Strongholds

"Come, let us return to the Lord. He will heal us. In just a short time, He will restore us, so that we may live in His presence" (Hosea 6:1-2 NLT)

Using This Discussion Guide

This is only a guide. This discussion guide contains too many questions for most groups to answer in a single session. You may choose a few questions from each section after considering the needs of your group.

A. OPEN YOUR SESSION WITH PRAYER

B. INTRODUCTION:

This Bible discussion covers the nine biblical principles of breaking free from destructive strongholds. Mike put them in an acrostic, making them easy to remember. They spell out B–R–E–A–K F–R–E–E. Henry David Thoreau said, "most people lead quiet lives of desperation." We, as Christians, need not be relegated to such a fate. Christ is our victor and healer. Victory over strongholds can come through these steps.

C. BIBLE DISCUSSION: PICK THE POINTS YOU WANT TO DISCUSS.

SECTION 1: PERSONALIZING THE MESSAGE

a) What insights from the message left the biggest impression on you? Why?
b) What encouraged or reassured you from the message?
c) What did you read that challenged or convicted you?
d) How did the message increase your appreciation for God the Father, Jesus Christ, or the Holy Spirit?
e) What positive result could occur from heeding the message or the painful consequences of disregarding its truth?

SECTION 2: DIGGING DEEPER

Ephesians 6:12: *"We are not fighting against flesh-and-blood enemies, but against evil rulers and authorities of the unseen world, against mighty powers in this dark world, and against evil spirits in the heavenly places"* (NLT).

- **From Ephesians 6:12, what are the sources of destructive strongholds?**

2 Corinthians 10:3-5: "3 We are human, but we don't wage war as humans do. 4 We use God's mighty weapons, not worldly weapons, to knock down the STRONGHOLDS of human reasoning and to destroy FALSE ARGUMENTS. 5 We destroy every PROUD OBSTACLE that keeps people from knowing God. We capture their REBELLIOUS THOUGHTS and teach them to obey Christ" (NLT).

- Using your imagination, what does waging "war as the humans do" look like, from 2 Corinthians 10:3?

- What are Satan's three tools for establishing strongholds in 2 Corinthians 10:3-15? What are your thoughts on these instruments?

- From verse 4, why should we use God's mighty weapons to conquer strongholds rather than worldly weapons?

- What should we do when confronted with these attacks (verses 4 & 5b)?

2 Corinthians 6:6-7: *"We prove ourselves by our purity, our understanding, our patience, our kindness, by the Holy Spirit within us, and by our sincere love. We faithfully preach the truth. God's power is working in us. We use the weapons of righteousness in the right hand for attack and the left hand for defense"* (NLT).

- What are the seven weapons mentioned in 2 Corinthians 6:6-7 that we can use to defeat strongholds?

- Describe how each weapon is powerful enough to destroy the enemies' strongholds.

B — BEGIN TODAY

Ecclesiastes 11:4 says, *"If you wait for perfect conditions, you'll never get anything done!"* (LB).

Mike shares, "Every day you procrastinate on changing a bad habit; it gets more deeply ingrained. Every day you put off changing the things you know should be changed in your life; they become more habitual and stronger with delay."

- What do Ecclesiastes 11:4 and Mike's teaching say to you? How would you apply this in your life?

R — REFUSE TO BLAME OTHERS

Mike cites a quote from Carlos Santana, "Most people don't have that willingness to break bad habits. They make a lot of excuses, and they talk like victims."

- Why is blaming everyone and everything for your unhappiness and problems counterproductive?

Proverbs 19:3: *"Some people ruin themselves by their own stupid actions, and they blame the Lord" (GN).*

- What are your thoughts on this Scripture?
- Why do you think accepting personal responsibility is essential for breaking bad habits?

E — EXAMINE MY LIFE

Lamentations 3:40: *"Let us examine our ways and test them and return to the Lord" (NIV).*

- What is the value of examining your life?
- Lamentations 3:40 implies that we are to examine our life against the ways of God. Why is it essential that we use God's standard versus the practices of this world?

Psalm 32:3-5 says, *"My dishonesty made me miserable, and it filled my days with frustration … until I finally admitted my sins and stopped trying to hide them. I said to myself, "I will confess them to the Lord." And You forgave me! All my sin is gone" (LB).*

- From Psalm 32:3-5, what happens when we pretend and hide our weaknesses?
- What should we do instead of being dishonest and in denial from Psalm 32:3-5?
- What happens when you confess your wrongs?

Mike teaches, "If you want to make any changes in your life, you must stop pretending. You must stop covering up your flaws because hiding a bad habit only strengthens its grip on you and causes it to grow deeper."

- What are your thoughts on this statement?

A — ASK CHRIST TO TAKE CONTROL OF MY LIFE

Colossians 1:17 says, *"In Christ, all things hold together"* (NIV).

- What are some of the things that can control you?
- What does Colossians 1:17 teach about Christ?

Mike shares, "Anything you center your life around that isn't Jesus Christ is your idol, and idols aren't strong enough to hold your life together.

- Do you agree with this statement? What are your thoughts on this?

Mike shares, "Freedom comes from choosing Christ as your master."

- What kind of freedom have you experienced from choosing Christ as your master?

Romans 6:12-13: *"Do not let sin control your body any longer; do not give in to its sinful desires ... but give yourselves COMPLETELY to God—every part of you ... to be used for His good purposes"* (LB)

- What are some destructive effects of sin?
- From Romans 6:12-13, what happens when you "give yourself completely to God—every part of you?

Mike shares the following practical steps to "give yourself completely to Christ to be used for His good purposes." (1) Pray daily (2) Read God's Word daily (3) Obey God moment by moment (4) Trust God for every detail of your life (5) Join a local Church and get involved —Attend weekly worship services and Bible Study or small group meetings (6) Serve in a ministry area where your gifts and passion could benefit others.

- Which of the following are you actively practicing and those that need improvement?

"God's power is very great for us who believe. That power is the same as the great strength God used to raise Christ from the dead and put Him at His right side in the heavenly world" (Ephesians 1:19-20 NCV).

- What does it mean to you that the same power that raised Christ from the dead is now available to you?
- Do you believe that resurrection power can deliver you from destructive strongholds?

K — KEEP AWAY FROM TEMPTATION

Proverbs 4:26-27: *"Plan carefully what you do, and whatever you do will turn out right. Avoid evil and walk straight ahead. Don't go one step off the right way"* (GN).

- According to Proverbs 4:26–27, how can you overcome evil?
- How can careful planning help you avoid the desire to fulfill a harmful habit?

Mike shares, "The secret to overcoming temptation is identifying your triggers, setting boundaries, and having a plan. Decide in advance that you're not going to give in. If you wait until you're in the tempting moment to decide what you'll do, you've already lost. Your emotions will swell up, your feelings will kick in, your senses will get overwhelmed, and you may struggle to resist the temptation."

- What are your thoughts on this statement?

Matthew 26:41: *"Keep watch and pray so that you will not give in to temptation. For the spirit is willing, but the body is weak!"* (NLT).

- From Matthew 26:41, what would strengthen you against temptation?
- Why should you not neglect prayer?

God says, *"Call on Me in the day of trouble; I will deliver you, and you will honor me"* (Psalm 50:15 NIV).

- From Psalm 50:15, what does God want you to do on the day of trouble?
- What does God promise to do when you call on Him?

Hebrews 2:18, 4:15: *"Because Jesus experienced temptation when He suffered, He is able to help others when they are tempted. He was tempted in every way that we are, but He didn't sin."* (GW).

- What thoughts come to mind when you read Hebrews 2:18 and 4:15?
- How does this Scripture encourage you to pray to Jesus for help resisting temptation?

F — FOCUS ON SOMETHING BETTER

Proverbs 4:23: "Be careful how you think. Your life is shaped by your thoughts" (GN).

- What is the warning in this verse?
- Why do you think your thoughts shape your life?
- What does this Scripture teach you about the quality of your thoughts?

Mike describes the *Principle of Replacement:* "The way you get rid of a wrong thought is to replace it with a good one. Basically, you reprogram your mind with new, honorable thought patterns based on God's Word to defeat the stronghold.

- What do you think about this statement?
- What experience do you have with this statement?

Philippians 4:8: *"Fill your mind with things that are good and deserve praise. Things that are true, noble, right, pure, lovely and honorable"* (GN).

- From Philippians 4:8, what does the Bible teach to fill your mind?
- What fits the criteria of Philippians 4:8 to fill our minds with?
- Share an example of how the Bible can defeat Satan's tools of stronghold— "false argument," "proud obstacles" that deny God's knowledge and power, and "rebellious thought."

R — RESTORE BROKEN RELATIONSHIPS

Romans 12:18: *"As far as your responsibility goes, live at peace with EVERYONE"* (PH)

- From Romans 12:18, what does God say is our responsibility?
- Who is included and not included in this command?

Mike shares, "Our bad habits hurt the people around us. We cause grief to others and guilt to ourselves. Anything out of control in your life hurts you and others."

- What are your thoughts on this statement?

James 5:16: *"Confess your sins to each other and pray for each other so that you may be healed"* (NIV).

- What does James 5:16 say will happen if you admit your faults to each other and pray?

- Why is it hard to admit our faults to someone else?
- Once you do admit your faults, how do you feel?

Mike describes that "telling another person about your faults releases the pressure valve. When you shine the light on your secrets and bad habits, suddenly, it loses its power over you. Our bad habits and secrets are where God wants to give us the most grace, mercy, and healing if we obey His instructions.

- What are your thoughts on this statement?

E — ENLIST SUPPORT

Mike suggests, "It would help if you sought outside assistance to encourage and hold you accountable. If you want to be what God intended for you in life, you can't do it alone because God didn't create you to be a "Lone Ranger." God never intended for you to go through life on your own."

- What are your thoughts on this statement?
- Think of someone who has supported you and share how they have been helpful to you.

Ecclesiastes 4:9-10: "Two are better off than one because TOGETHER ... if one of them falls down, the other can help him up. But if someone is alone and falls... there's no one to help him" (GN)

- From Ecclesiastes 4:9–10, how are two better off than one?
- How do you think a partner could help you face temptation?
- Has a friend or loved one ever helped you through a difficult time? How did having that person's help during a difficult time benefit you?

Mike describes, "Habits of self-harm become more ingrained and difficult to break when an individual lacks access to a supportive social network. You must have support. When people are isolated from a supportive community, destructive behavior patterns become entrenched and difficult to change. People continue to fall into the same destructive cycle because they try to do it on their own."

- What are your thoughts on this statement?
- Who would you turn to for support? Who would you recommend someone turn to for help?

E — EXTEND MYSELF TO HELP OTHERS

2 Corinthians 1:4: *"Christ helps us in all our troubles so that we are able to help others in trouble, using the same help that we ourselves have received from God"* (GN).

- How does knowing that Christ is your helper in all your troubles feel?
- What does this Scripture passage teach you?
- Can you give examples of how God helped you through your trials?
- From 2 Corinthians 1:4, what is one reason God may allow you to go through suffering?
- What are some examples of how you can "help others in need?"
- How do you feel about stepping forward to help others in need "with the same help you have received from God"?

1 Corinthians 10:13 *"God keeps His promise, and He will not allow you to be tested beyond your power to remain firm; at the time you are put to the test, He will give you the strength to endure it and so provide you with a way out"* (GN).

- What words or ideas stand out to you in 1 Corinthians 10:13?

- What does this Scripture passage teach you?
- What does 1 Corinthians 10:13 say God will never allow to happen to you?
- How does this verse encourage you when you feel pushed to your limit?

SECTION 3: PERSONAL APPLICATION AND COMMITMENT

To break free of negative controlling behavior, you must: Begin now; Refuse to blame other people; Examine your life; Ask God to take complete control; Keep away from temptation; Focus on something better; work to Restore broken relationships, Enlist support, and finally, Extend myself to help others.

a) What personal application has the Lord shown you from this message?
b) How do you feel about following through with it?

D. PRAYER POINTS

1. Pray that you and the other members of your Small Group will respond positively to this message and will act on it.
2. Pray for a miraculous outcome as you and your group put this wisdom into practice.
3. Ask everyone in the group to share what they need prayer for, and then pray for those requests.
4. Request that one of your members lead in a closing prayer.

PLEASE REACH OUT TO ANYONE WHO DID NOT MAKE IT TO YOUR MEETING

Chapter 7—What It Takes to Be a Great Leader—The 8 Cs of Influential Leadership

Using This Discussion Guide

This is only a guide. This discussion guide contains too many questions for most groups to answer in a single session. You may choose a few questions from each section after considering the needs of your group.

A. OPEN YOUR SESSION WITH PRAYER

B. INTRODUCTION:

This Bible discussion explores the life of Nehemiah and identifies the eight in-demand, indispensable qualities of influential leaders to encourage you to be the leader you were created to be.

D. BIBLE DISCUSSION: PICK THE POINTS YOU WANT TO DISCUSS.

SECTION 1: PERSONALIZING THE MESSAGE

a) What insights from the message left the biggest impression on you? Why?
b) What encouraged or reassured you from the message?
c) What did you read that challenged or convicted you?
d) How did the message increase your appreciation for God?

e) What advantage could occur from heeding the message or the painful consequences of disregarding its truth?

SECTION 2: DIGGING DEEPER

Mike begins the chapter with this statement, "Nothing happens until someone provides leadership for it!"

- What are your thoughts on this statement?

- Share a positive outcome that occurred because you or someone took the lead.

Mike describes a biblical leader as "Someone with God-given ability and responsibility to influence a group of people to accomplish God's purposes. Christians are called to reflect Christ's glory in our environments to influence society. You are a leader in your family, home, work, and school. God places us where He needs us to exemplify authentic leadership."

- Are you in agreement or disagreement with this teaching? Why? or why not?

- How does this statement inspire you to take on leadership responsibilities?

Deuteronomy 28:13: *"The LORD will make you the head, not the tail. If you pay attention to the commands of the LORD your God that I give you this day and carefully follow them, you will always be at the top, never at the bottom" (NIV).*

- What does God promise in Deuteronomy 28:13?

- What actions are required of you concerning this promise?

- Why do you think God makes obedience a requirement for success?

Paul told Timothy (and to every believer), *"Be an example and set a pattern for the believers in speech, in conduct, in love, in faith, and in moral purity"* (1 Timothy 4:12 AMP).

- Briefly share an example of someone who demonstrated positive behavior that influenced you.
- What behaviors are you demonstrating as an influential leader in your home, work, school, or church?

THE 8 Cs OF INFLUENTIAL LEADERSHIP

Mike cites this study from Harvard Business Review: "Compassion is the intent to contribute to the happiness and well-being of others. A compassionate leader is genuinely interested in seeing their people perform and thrive. Compassionate leaders appear stronger and have more engaged followers."

- What stands out to you from this study from Harvard Business Review?
- What compassionate leader comes to mind who has had an impact on you? Why?
- Why do you think compassionate leaders attract engaged followers?
- What compassionate leadership qualities do you practice or hope to practice?

1. COMPASSION

Read an example of Nehemiah's compassion: *"The earlier governors—those preceding me—placed a heavy burden ... and took advantage of the people. But BECAUSE I FEARED THE LORD, I DID NOT ACT THAT WAY ... I asked for nothing, even though I regularly fed 150 Jewish officials at my table, besides all the visitors from other lands! The provisions I paid for each day included one ox, six choice sheep or goats, and a large number of poultry"* (Nehemiah 5:15-18 NIV+NLT).

- How did Nehemiah demonstrate compassionate leadership in Nehemiah 5:16-18?
- What was Nehemiah's motivation?
- How does the fear of the Lord make you a compassionate person?
- What practical actions can you practice to demonstrate compassion to people?

Nehemiah was furious about injustice, manipulation, and bullying. He states, *"When I heard their outcry and these charges, I was very angry"* Nehemiah 5:6 *(NIV)*. Mike suggests, "We must be angry at social injustice when the powerful manipulate and hurt the innocent. This is righteous indignation. Nehemiah's anger was evidence of his compassion for people."

- What are your thoughts on Mike's statement?
- Can anger ever be a loving reaction? If so, what instances?

Mike shares, "Leadership without love is manipulation. Leadership with love is compassion. Great leaders care about people!"

- What are your thoughts on this statement?

2. CONTEMPLATION

Mike explains contemplation as "reviewing, reflecting, meditating, and considering matters before speaking or acting."

- How can practicing contemplation support your success, or how can it hinder your success?

Nehemiah 1:5-6: "Then I said, 'Lord, God of heaven, the great and awesome God, who keeps His covenant of love with those that love Him and obey His commands, let your ear be attentive and your eyes open to hear the prayer your servant is PRAYING BEFORE YOU DAY AND NIGHT for your servants, the people of Israel'" (NIV).

- Who does Nehemiah pray for in Nehemiah 1:5-6?
- As a leader, why is it crucial that you pray constantly?
- Who, specifically, should you be praying for? What should you be praying for them?

Mike describes Nehemiah contemplating, surveying, reflecting, and talking to the Lord while riding around the city at night and observing the destruction. He was going over in his mind what was going on and what he needed to do.

Nehemiah 2:11-16: "I went to Jerusalem, and after staying there three days, I set out during the night ... examining the walls of Jerusalem, which had been broken down, and its gates, which had been destroyed by fire ... The officials did not know where I had gone or what I was doing, because as yet I had said Nothing to the officials or any others who would be doing the work" (NIV)

- Why is it critical for leaders to examine situations before acting?
- What leadership lessons from Nehemiah 2:11-16 can you apply in your own life?

3. CHEERFULNESS

Mike points out, "Cheerfulness is one of the essential qualities of a leader. No one follows a pessimist, at least for long. Influential leaders are encouragers, not discouragers. The job of leadership is to lift people, not let them down."

- What are your thoughts on this statement?

Paul teaches, *"Always be joyful. Never stop praying. Be thankful in all circumstances, for this is God's will for you who belong to Christ Jesus"* (1 Thessalonians 5:16-18 NLT).

- What is the message of 1 Thessalonians 5:16–18?
- Why do you think prayer and gratitude make people joyful?
- What are some things you can be thankful for in all circumstances?

Nehemiah tells people who are feeling oppressed and worn out, *"This is a sacred day before our Lord. Don't be dejected and sad, for the joy of the Lord is your strength!"* (Nehemiah 8:10 NLT).

- From Nehemiah 8:10, where does joy come from?
- What is the difference between happiness and joy?
- Why do you think Nehemiah encouraged depressed people to choose joy?
- How does cheerfulness support a winning mindset?

4. CONCENTRATION

Mike shares, "Influential leaders can zero in on a problem and stick with it until it is resolved. Success is impossible without the self-control to focus on an objective for an extended period of time. Success necessitates maintaining sustained concentration on a specific goal or task."

- What are your thoughts on this statement?
- Share an example of how you demonstrated concentration to achieve an outcome.

Mike shares an example of Nehemiah's concentration in handling distractions from the opposition: *"Sanballat and Geshem sent me this message, 'Come let us meet together on the plain of Ono.' But they were scheming to harm me. So I sent messengers to them with this reply.*

'I am carrying on a great project and cannot go down. Why should the work stop while I leave it and go down to you?' Four times they sent me the same message, and I gave them the same answer each time" (Nehemiah 6:2-4 NIV).

Nehemiah knew these guys were trying to distract and derail the project and harm him by proposing sham meetings.

- What are your thoughts on Nehemiah's ability to focus on the task at hand without becoming distracted?
- What can you learn from Nehemiah's example of focus?

5 CREATIVITY

Mike shares, "Influential Leaders are creative change agents. They are never afraid to make the required changes to get the task on track."

- What are your thoughts on this statement?
- Can you think of an obsolete product or company? In your opinion, what made customers dislike them?
- Why do you think people resist change? What happens if we are resistant to change?
- Share a change you made in your life that resulted in a positive outcome.

Mike explains, As the enemies planned a surprise attack on the workers while they were at work, Nehemiah devised a creative problem-solving strategy:

"Our enemies said, 'Before they know it or see us, we will be right there among them and will kill them and put an end to the work.' Therefore I stationed some of the people behind the lowest points of the wall at the exposed places, posting them by families, with their swords, spears, and bows" (Nehemiah 4:11,13 NIV).

"I stood up and said to the... people, "Don't be afraid of them. Remember the Lord, who is great and awesome, and fight for your families, your sons and your daughters, your wives, and your homes ... From that day on, half of the men did the work while the other half were equipped with spears, shields, bows and armor" (Nehemiah 4:14-16 NIV).

- From Nehemiah 4:11-16, what do you think Nehemiah was trying to accomplish?
- What does the expression, "If life gives you a lemon, you make lemonade," mean to you?
- What can you learn from Nehemiah's example of creativity?

6. COURAGE

Mike shares: "Courage is the willingness to take risks and step out on faith. It is not the absence of fear, but rather moving forward despite your fear, trusting in the Lord."

- What does this teaching mean to you?

Mike describes three examples of Nehemiah's courage in this section of the chapter (Refer to this section)

1. When asking the king for permission (Nehemiah 2:2)
2. When responding to enemy attacks (Nehemiah 4:14)
3. When confronting corruption (Nehemiah 5:7-13)

- Review Mike's comments on the above situations from the Chapter. What are your thoughts on Nehemiah's courage in the above situations?
- What can you learn from Nehemiah's example of creativity?

7. CLEAR CONSCIENCE (INTEGRITY)

Mike shares, "Integrity refers to honesty, trustworthiness, and reliability. Leaders with integrity act according to their words (i.e., they practice what they preach). They own up to their mistakes instead of hiding them, blaming others, or making excuses. Integrity also involves being law-abiding, following your company's policies, being courteous, and respectful of others.

- What are your thoughts on this statement?
- What happens if we do not act with integrity?

Mike shares, "A leader's behavior reflects not only on their own reputation but also on the reputation of their group and family."

- What example can you share of how a leader's behavior positively or negatively affected their family or group?
- How does this teaching influence your choices and actions?

Mike points out that "when you become a success, three things come with it—power, prestige, and privilege. The temptation is to abuse all three. Nehemiah didn't do that. He states, *"Those governors before me made life difficult for the people by taking food, wine, and one pound of silver from them. Even the governors' servants took advantage of their power over the people. But I didn't do that because I feared God"* (Nehemiah 5:15b NLT).

- Why do you think leaders abuse their power, prestige, and privilege?
- From Nehemiah 5:15, why do you think the governor's servants followed the corruption of their leaders?
- What kind of environment does corruption foster in a family, church, or society?
- What does Nehemiah 5:15 say about Nehemiah's integrity?

- What was Nehemiah's motivation for not following his predecessor's actions?
- What can you learn from Nehemiah's example of integrity?

8. CONVICTION

Mike shares, "Great leaders have strong convictions that enable them to persevere through transitions and challenges to carry out their plans."

- What are your thoughts on this statement?
- What non-negotiable convictions do you hold? Why?

Mike points out Satan's Eight Pressure Schemes from the Nehemiah narrative as *derision, discouragement, dread, division, discord, distraction, defamation, and danger.*

- How does this revelation help you defend yourself against these attacks?
- Share any experience you may have had with any of these destructive tactics, and what is your best practical advice to overcome them?

Mike shares: Nehemiah based his convictions on four things: (1) He had a *compelling purpose.* He was convinced God had called him to do this great project and would not be distracted. (2) He had a *clear perspective.* He asked God for wisdom. (3) He had a *continual prayer.* He prayed continually about everything. (4). He had a *courageous persistence.* He kept on keeping on, despite the opposition.

- Which of the four convictions in italics above is/are most comfortable, and which are difficult for you and why?

- What can you learn from Nehemiah's example of conviction?

"The wall was finished just 52 days after we had begun. When our enemies and the surrounding nations heard about it, they were frightened and humiliated. They realized this work had been done with the help of our God" (Nehemiah 6:15-16 NLT)

- From Nehemiah 6:15-16, what was Nehemiah's enemies' reaction to the finished project despite their relentless opposition?
- From Nehemiah 6:15-16, what was the chief reason for the project's speedy completion?
- What does this episode reveal about your enemies versus God's help?
- What has God revealed to you from this Scripture passage to encourage you about your challenges?

SECTION 3. SELF EVALUATION

With these eight leadership values we see in Nehemiah's life, Mike recommends you take time for self-evaluation. Ask yourself these four questions:

- Which of these eight-character qualities are strongest in your life? Compassion, contemplation, cheerfulness, concentration, creativity, courage, clear consciousness, and conviction.
- Which of these character qualities is weakest?
- Working on something is hard if you haven't clearly identified it. What character qualities would you like to develop the most?
- What could you do this week to practice demonstrating this quality? Is there a project you

could think of this week or a situation you might best demonstrate the quality you want to work on?

- Force yourself to make an application.

D. PRAYER POINTS

1. Pray that you and the other members of your Small Group will respond positively to this message and will act on it.
2. Pray for a miraculous outcome as you and your group put this wisdom into practice.
3. Ask everyone in the group to share what they need prayer for, and then pray for those requests.
4. Request that one of your members lead in a closing prayer.

PLEASE REACH OUT TO ANYONE WHO DID NOT
MAKE IT TO YOUR MEETING

Chapter 8—How to Live a Life of Significance

"Jabez was the most respected member of his family" (1 Chronicles 4:9 GN)

Using This Discussion Guide

This is only a guide. This discussion guide contains too many questions for most groups to answer in a single session. You may choose a few questions from each section after considering the needs of your group.

A. OPEN YOUR SESSION WITH PRAYER

B. INTRODUCTION:

Jabez was easily identifiable in a crowd. God chose him specifically out of more than 600 people. Just what was it about Jabez that set him apart? Drawing on lessons from Jabez's life, this Bible study explores how we can achieve the life of significance that God has for us.

C. BIBLE DISCUSSION: PICK THE POINTS YOU WANT TO DISCUSS.

SECTION 1: PERSONALIZING THE MESSAGE

a) What insights from the message left the biggest impression on you? Why?

b) What encouraged or reassured you from the message?

c) What did you read that challenged or convicted you?

d) What positive result could occur from heeding the message or the painful consequences of disregarding its truth?

SECTION 2: DIGGING DEEPER

"Jabez was more honorable than his brothers. His mother had named him Jabez, saying, "I gave birth to him in pain." Jabez cried out to the God of Israel, "Oh, that you would bless me and enlarge my territory! Let your hand be with me, and keep me from harm so that I will be free from pain." And God granted his request" (1 Chronicles 4:9-10 NIV).

1. YOU NEED GREAT AMBITION IF YOU WANT TO LIVE A SIGNIFICANT LIFE

Mike cites Brian Tracy, *"All successful people are big dreamers. They imagine what their future could be—ideal in every respect—and then they work every day toward their distant vision, goal or purpose."*

- Does this statement reflect your life ambition and ethic? Why or why not?
- Share a situation where setting and pursuing a goal helped you accomplish your dream.

1 Chronicles 4:9: *"Jabez cried out to God ... Oh, that you would bless me and enlarge my territory!"* (NIV).

- What requests did Jabez make of God?
- What do 1 Chronicles 4:9 say to you about Jabez's ambition?

Mike describes, "Jabez is an example of the power of thinking big and trusting God. Great men and women are simply ordinary people with great ideas, ambitions, and dreams. If you want to be like Jabez, you need to say, "Lord, bless me and enlarge my territory! God, I want you to do something significant in my life."

- How do this statement and Jabez's prayer request inspire you to be ambitious in your prayer requests and aspirations?

2. YOU NEED A GROWING FAITH IF YOU WANT TO LIVE A SIGNIFICANT LIFE

Mike mentions in the Jabez narrative, "There's no mention of any unique ability, talent, or gift that he possessed. He was an ordinary person with an uncommon faith in God. Without a doubt, God uses ordinary people. There is something more important than education, ability, talent, gifts, financial status, and background. It's faith! Believing God can produce incredible outcomes in your life."

- What thoughts come to your mind based on this statement?
- What examples can you share about ordinary people who accomplished incredible outcomes because of their faith in God?
- How does this lesson encourage you to live out your faith?

Mike shares, "You need a growing faith to accomplish more incredible things beyond your age, education, race, and even adversity."

- What are your thoughts on this statement?
- What personal experience can you share concerning this statement?

Mike describes three kinds of mindsets in life: *Accusers, Excusers, and Choosers.*

- From the chapter, how do you describe these three mindsets?
- Which mindset do you adopt and why?

3. A GENUINE PRAYER LIFE IS REQUIRED TO LIVE A SIGNIFICANT LIFE

Mike shares, "Here is a guy whose name means he has a destiny of pain but experienced the opposite in his life by being more prosperous than anyone in his generation. This turn-around is attributable to his prayer to God for the blessings of territorial expansion, divine active presence, and deliverance from all trouble."

- What does this statement mean to you?
- What lesson can you draw from Jabez's turn-around?

I. Jabez Prayed for God's Power in His Life

1 Chronicles 4:10: "Jabez cried out to God ... "Oh, that you would bless me and enlarge my territory!" (NIV).

Mike shares, "Jabez knew to live above average, he needed God's power to accomplish his dream. He couldn't do it all by himself. He prayed with a clear, specific goal in mind. He says, "God, I want you to give me real estate and expand my holdings."

- What lesson can you draw from Jabez's prayer in 1 Chronicles 4:10 and Mike's statement?
- Why do you need to be specific in your prayer requests?

James 4:3: "When you ask, you do not receive, because you ask with wrong motives, that you may spend what you get on your pleasures" (NIV).

- From James 4:3, what is a condition for answered prayer?

- What is an example of praying with the wrong motive?
- Mike shares, "God never honors an unworthy motive." Why?

Ephesians 3:20: "With God's power working in us, God can do much, much more than anything we can ask or imagine" (NCV).

- What stands out to you about Ephesians 3:20?
- From Ephesians 3:20, what can God do?
- Where does God's power work, according to Ephesians 3:20?
- What does this Scripture teach you?
- How does this truth influence your prayer requests?

Jeremiah 33:3: "Call unto me, and I will answer you and show you great and mighty things, which you do not know" (NKJV).

- What phrases or thoughts jump out at you from Jeremiah 33:3?
- What does this Scripture teach you?
- According to Jeremiah 33:3, what must you do?
- What does God promise to do in response to our actions in Jeremiah 33:3?
- What is your response to this truth?

II. Jabez Prayed for God's Presence in His Life

1 Chronicles 4:10: "Let your hand be with me" (NIV)

Mike points out, "Growth brings with it more pressure and responsibilities. The larger territory you have, the more enemies will envy you. The more you grow in your relationship with the Lord, the more the devil will bother you."

- What are your thoughts on this statement?

- How does God's presence make a difference in your life?
- What experience do you have with this statement?

III. Jabez Prayed for God's Protection in His Life

1 Chronicles 4:10: *"Lord ... keep me from harm so that I will be free from pain"* (NIV).

- Why is it essential to pray for protection?
- What thoughts come to mind about Nadin Khoury's story from the chapter? What applications can you draw from the account?

Read the following Scriptures:

"You, O LORD, are always my shield from danger; You give me victory and restore my courage" (Psalm 3:3 GNT).

"God gives power to the weak and strength to the powerless" (Isaiah 40:29 NLT).

"Even those who are young grow weak; young people can fall exhausted. But those who trust in the Lord for help will find their strength renewed. They will rise on wings like eagles; they will run and not get weary; they will walk and not grow weak" (Isaiah 40:30-31 GNT)

"Look to the Lord and his strength; seek His face always" (1 Chronicles 16:11 NIV)

- What verse, words, or ideas jump out to you?
- What do you think is the common theme in these Scripture passages?
- What encourages you about these promises?

"For God has RESCUED us from the kingdom of darkness and TRANSFERRED us into the Kingdom of His dear Son, who

PURCHASED our freedom with His blood and FORGAVE our sins" (Colossians 1:13-14 NLT with margin).

- In Colossians 1:13-14 the precious gift of salvation is expressed in 4 verbs that God has done for us in Christ Jesus—rescued, transferred, purchased, forgave. Replace the words "us" and "our" with "me" and "my" and read that aloud.
- How does this Scripture passage increase your appreciation for God the Father and Jesus Christ?

SECTION 3: PERSONAL APPLICATION AND COMMITMENT

Jabez knew he didn't need to fear anything with God's power, presence, and protection. When you combine the powerful forces of great ambition, a growing faith, and a genuine prayer life, you can be sure you will stand out in a crowd and live an above-average life of significance.

a) What personal application has the Lord shown you from the message?

b) How do you feel about following through with it?

D. PRAYER POINTS

1. Pray that you and the other members of your Small Group will respond positively to this message and will act on it.
2. Pray for a miraculous outcome as you and your group put this wisdom into practice.
3. Ask everyone in the group to share what they need prayer for, and then pray for those requests.
4. Request that one of your members lead in a closing prayer.

PLEASE REACH OUT TO ANYONE WHO DID NOT MAKE IT TO YOUR MEETING

Chapter 9—How to Overcome Your Weakness to Become a Stronger Person

"I want to remind you that your strength must come from the Lord's mighty power within you" (Ephesians 6:10 LB)

Using This Discussion Guide

This is only a guide. This discussion guide contains too many questions for most groups to answer in a single session. You may choose a few questions from each section after considering the needs of your group.

A. OPEN YOUR SESSION WITH PRAYER

B. INTRODUCTION:

This Bible discussion explores the life of Samson from Judges chapters 14 through 16 to point out three characteristics to avoid and corresponding principles to adopt so we will be stronger people.

C. BIBLE DISCUSSION: PICK THE POINTS YOU WANT TO DISCUSS.

SECTION 1: PERSONALIZING THE MESSAGE

a) What insights from the message left the biggest impression on you? Why?

b) What encouraged or reassured you from the message?

c) What did you read that challenged or convicted you?

d) How did the message increase your appreciation for God the Father, Jesus Christ, or the Holy Spirit?

e) What positive result could occur from heeding the message or the painful consequences of disregarding its truth?

SECTION 2: DIGGING DEEPER

Ephesians 6:10-11: "Your strength must come from the Lord's mighty power within you. Put on all of God's armor so that you'll be able to stand against Satan's strategies and tricks." (LB).

- Mike shares, "You better believe Satan has a boatload of "strategies and tricks" to sap your strength. They are calculated tactics designed to weaken you." What are some of Satan's bag of tricks you have experienced in your life or the life of others?

- From Ephesians 6:10-11, what words or ideas jump out to you?

- From Ephesians 6:10-11, how can we overcome Satan's strategies?

1. AN UNDISCIPLINED LIFESTYLE WILL WEAKEN YOUR LIFE.

LESSON #1: TO BE A STRONG PERSON, I MUST DISCIPLINE MY DESIRES AND LIVE BY GODLY PRINCIPLES RATHER THAN PLEASURE

Judges 14:1-4: *"Samson went down to Timnah and saw there a young Philistine woman. When he returned, he said to his father and mother, 'I have seen a Philistine woman in Timnah; now GET HER FOR ME AS MY WIFE.' His father and mother replied, 'Isn't there an acceptable woman among your relatives or among all our people? Must you go to the uncircumcised Philistines to get a wife?' But Samson said to his father, 'Get her for me. SHE'S THE RIGHT ONE FOR ME'"* (NIV).

Mike points out, "God told Samson not to marry an unbeliever. His parents warned him not to do it, and he vowed not to marry an unbeliever. But when he saw this woman, his convictions went out the door. He said, 'I've got to have her!'

- If single, do you have any rules about whom you can date? Or if married, what dating advice would you give an unmarried person? Why?
- Why are the risks of following through with a marriage commitment based on "love at first sight only."
- Why do you think it is unwise to marry an unbeliever?

Galatians 6:7-8: "Don't be misled; remember that YOU CAN'T IGNORE GOD AND GET AWAY WITH IT; a man will always reap just the kind of crop he sows! If he sows to please his own wrong desires, he will be planting seeds of evil and will surely reap a harvest of spiritual decay and death" (LB).

- What is God saying to you from Galatians 6:7-8?

Mike shares, "The lesson from Samson's first mistake is we must learn to make decisions based on principles rather than pleasure. Otherwise, we'll do the convenient and pleasurable things, not necessarily the right thing. Strong people disciple their desires and live by godly principles rather than pleasure."

- What are your thoughts on this statement?
- Share a potential consequence of making decisions based on pleasure rather than principles.

1 Peter 4:1-2: "Strengthen yourselves with the way of thinking that (Christ) had ... LIVE YOUR LIVES CONTROLLED BY GOD'S WILL, NOT BY HUMAN DESIRES" (GN).

- From 1 Peter 4:1-2, why is living our lives controlled by God's standards essential?
- 1 Peter 4:1-2 implies we weaken ourselves when operating outside God's will. Why is God's thoughts more effective than human desires?

Proverbs 25:28: "A person without self-control is like a city with broken-down walls" (NLT).

- What specific examples or images come to your mind from Proverbs 25:28?
- What does Proverbs 25:28 say about an undisciplined life?
- How does an undisciplined lifestyle (carelessness) weaken your life? How does disciplining my life by living by godly standards make me stronger?

2. RESENTMENT WILL WEAKEN YOUR LIFE

LESSON #2: TO BE A STRONGER PERSON, I MUST RESTRAIN MY REACTIONS WHEN THINGS GO WRONG.

Mike describes the loss of Samson's bride prompted him to go out and catch 300 foxes, tied them by their tails and lit them. This started a fire that burned the vineyards, olive groves, and farmhouses, robing the Philistines of their food supply (Judges 15:3). The Philistines returned his revenge with a vengeance by burning Samson's bride and her father to death (Judges 15:6). Samson retaliated by attacking the Philistines and viciously slaughtered 1,000 of them (Judges 15:15).

- What does Samson do when he loses his wife due to his instability? (Judges 15:3-5)
- What do the Philistines do after Samson burns their crops? (Judges 15:6)
- How does Samson avenge this act? (Judges 15:7-8, 15)
- What happens when people resort to revenge?
- What do you learn from Samson's display of revenge?

Read the following scriptures:

Proverbs 29:22: "People with quick tempers cause a lot of quarreling and trouble" (GN).

Job 5:2: "To worry yourself to death with RESENTMENT would be a FOOLISH, SENSELESS thing to do" (GN).

Job 18:4: "You are only HURTING YOURSELF with your anger!" (GN)

- What does the Bible teach about resentment and revenge from the above Scriptures?

Mike points out that (1) Resentment wastes time because you're caught up in the past. (2) When you're resentful, it drains you of energy. It makes you miserable. (3) It wastes creativity. Sometimes we're so creative, thinking of ways to get back at the person who hurt us, that creativity is spent negatively rather than positively.

- What are your thoughts on this statement?
- How does harboring resentment weaken your life? And how is restraining your reactions when things go wrong a better option?

3. CARELESSNESS WILL WEAKEN YOUR LIFE (Judges 16:1-20)

LESSON #3: TO BE A STRONGER PERSON, I MUST HONOR MY COMMITMENTS EVEN WHEN I DON'T FEEL LIKE KEEPING THEM

Mike shares, "Samson made commitments to God, which was the chief reason for his exceptional strength. He took a Nazirite vow early in his life, which means he was never to drink alcohol his entire life. He was not to defile himself by contact with a dead body and never cut his hair. These stipulations were a daily reminder that he belonged to God, which was the source of his strength. But Samson hardly abstained from strong drinks and was often found in contact with the dead. He partially concerned himself with the uncut hair regulation, which he tragically ignored by concession at the end.

- What thoughts do you have about Samson's carelessness regarding his commitments?
- What happens when we are careless about our commitments to God, family, and employer?

Read the following scriptures:

Proverbs 18:20: *"You will have to live with the CONSEQUENCES of everything you say"* (GN).

1 Thessalonians 5:22: *"Abstain from ALL APPEARANCE of evil"* (KJV).

- How important is it to heed these cautions from God?

Judges 16:15-17: *"Then Delilah said to him, 'How can you say, 'I love you,' when you won't confide in me? This is the third time you have made a fool of me and haven't told me the secret of your great strength.' With such nagging, she prodded him day after day until he was sick to death of it. SO,*

SAMSON TOLD HER EVERYTHING. 'No razor has ever been used on my head,' he said, 'because I have been a Nazirite dedicated to God from my mother's womb. If my head were shaved, my strength would leave me, and I would become as weak as any other man'" (NIV).

- From Judges 16:15-17, how many times did Samson lie to Delilah before telling her his hair was the source of his strength?
- Does it suggest that Samson had reservations about Delilah's loyalty?
- Why is it helpful to keep your essential secrets from people who are not trustworthy?
- Have you experienced someone betraying your confidence by sharing your painful secrets without your approval? How did you view the relationship afterward?
- Why is keeping secrets important to maintaining your relationships?

Romans 8:13: "If you use your lives to do the wrong things your sinful selves want, you will die spiritually. But if you use the Spirit's help to stop doing the wrong things you do with your body, you will have true life" (NCV).

- From Romans 8:13, what is the consequence of doing wrong things?
- According to Romans 8:13, how can we stop doing wrong things?
- From Romans 8:13, what is the benefit of doing the right things?

Psalm 15:4b: *"Those who honor the Lord keep their promises to their neighbors, EVEN WHEN IT HURTS"* (NCV)

- Notice the Bible phrase, "even when it hurts." Why do you think God wants you to keep your commitments to people, not just when it is convenient but out of principle?
- How does carelessness weaken your life? And how does honoring your commitments a better option for being a stronger person?

Read the following Bible verses:

Ecclesiastes 7:8: "The end of a thing is better than its beginning" (NKJV)

John 4:34: Jesus: "My food is to do the will of Him who sent Me, and to finish His work" (NKJV)

- What is the Lord saying to you from the above Scripture passages?

SECTION 3: PERSONAL COMMITMENT AND APPLICATION

a) Consider adopting these three principles to become a stronger person (1) Discipline my desires and life by godly standards rather than pleasure. (2) Restrain my reactions whenever I am criticized or things go wrong, and (3) Honor my commitments even when I don't feel like keeping them.

b) What personal application has the Lord shown you from the message? How do you feel about following through with it?

D. PRAYER POINTS

1. Pray that you and the other members of your Small Group will respond positively to this message and will act on it.
2. Pray for a miraculous outcome as you and your group put this wisdom into practice.

3. Ask everyone in the group to share what they need prayer for, and then pray for those requests.
4. Request that one of your members lead in a closing prayer.

PLEASE REACH OUT TO ANYONE WHO DID NOT
MAKE IT TO YOUR MEETING

Chapter 10—How to Recover From Your Hurts

"God heals the brokenhearted and binds up their wounds" (Psalm 147:3 NIV)

Using This Discussion Guide

This is only a guide. This discussion guide contains too many questions for most groups to answer in a sing session. You may choose a few questions from each section after considering the needs of your group.

A. OPEN YOUR SESSION WITH PRAYER

B. INTRODUCTION:

Life is hard! Some people give up after a major life crisis and resign to a minimal existence. Other people rebound from life problems with fantastic resilience. Where can you get that courage to bounce back when your life falls apart? This Bible Study discussion will examine how Job overcame tragedies to help teach and prepare you to overcome difficulties, so we can come out victorious.

C. BIBLE DISCUSSION: PICK THE POINTS YOU WANT TO DISCUSS.

SECTION 1: PERSONALIZING THE MESSAGE

a) What insights from the message left the biggest impression on you? Why?

b) What encouraged or reassured you from the message?

c) What did you read that challenged or convicted you?

d) How did the message increase your appreciation for God the Father, Jesus Christ, or the Holy Spirit?

e) What positive result could occur from heeding the message or the painful consequences of disregarding its truth?

SECTION 2: DIGGING DEEPER

2 Corinthians 12:7-10: *"To keep me from being puffed up with pride because of the many wonderful things I saw, I was given a painful physical ailment ... Three times I prayed to the Lord about this and asked Him to take it away. But His answer was: "My grace is all you need, for My power is greatest when you are weak." I am most happy, then, to be proud of my weaknesses, in order to feel the protection of Christ's power over me. I am content with weaknesses, insults, hardships, persecutions, and difficulties for Christ's sake. For when I am weak, then I am strong"* (GN).

- What do you notice about 2 Corinthians 12:7-10?

- What words or ideas jump out to you?

- What does this Scripture passage teach you?

- Paul was stricken with a painful physical ailment and prayed to God 3 times to take it away. What was God's answer?

- In what ways did Paul experience God's grace and power during his painful sickness?

- Share a time when you experienced God's grace during a major problem.

Mike points out, "The secret to surviving a hurt is who and what you trust in. Put your trust in Jesus and His Promises."

- What are the consequences of trusting your job, finances, or a friend?
- What are the benefits of placing your trust in God?
- Describe the emotional state of someone who trusts in people and things versus someone who trusts God in difficult times.

John 16:33: Jesus: "By trusting Me, you will be unshakable and assured, deeply at peace. In this godless world, you will continue to experience difficulties. But take heart! I've conquered the world" (MSG).

- From John 16:33, what is Jesus saying to you?
- How could this Scripture encourage you or a friend in difficult times?

Job 36:15-16: *"Hard times and trouble are God's way of getting our attention! And at that very moment, God deeply desires to lead you from trouble and to spread your table with your favorite food"* (CEV).

- From Job 36:15-16, what words or ideas jump out to you
- From Job 36:15-16, when you face challenging times and trouble, what three things is God doing in your life?
- What does this Scripture mean to you personally?

THE EXAMPLE OF JOB—HOW TO RECOVER FROM YOUR HURTS

1. TELL GOD YOUR FEELINGS AND FRUSTRATIONS

Job 1:20: *"Job stood up, tore his robe in grief, and shaved his head. Then he fell to the ground and worshipped"* (GW).

- Most people pull back from God when they encounter a major problem. According to the example of Job, what should you do instead?

Lamentations 2:19: *"Rise during the night and cry out. Pour out your hearts like water to the Lord"* (NLT).

- How would you talk to God according to Lamentations 2:19?
- Personal Reflection: Take some time and tell God exactly how you feel about a difficult situation in your life. Make your prayer an act of worship by trusting God with your feelings.

Psalm 32:3: *"When I kept things to myself, I felt weak deep inside me. I moaned all day long"* (NCV).

- What do you think happens if we keep our hurts to ourselves rather than telling God?
- From Psalm 32:3, use your imagination to describe what is happening in this person's life.
- What was your experience when you kept a painful hurt inside you?

Hebrews 5:7: *"While Jesus lived on earth, He prayed to God and asked God for help. He prayed with loud cries and tears to the One who could save Him from death, and His prayer was heard because He trusted God"* (NCV).

- What do you notice about Hebrews 5:7?
- What does this Scripture passage teach you?
- Most people hold back from sharing their painful feelings with God. How does Jesus' example in Hebrews 5:7 teach you to come to God with your problems?
- What do you think will happen when you share your hurt feelings with God?

2. PRAISE GOD DESPITE YOUR CIRCUMSTANCES

Mike describes: "In every moment of your life, you have both good and bad at the time. So, no matter how good things are in your life, there's something not-so-great going on. And no matter how bad things are in your life, there is always something you can be thankful for."

- Reflect on this teaching and share an example of how this is realistic in your life.

Job 1:21-22: *"I was naked when I was born, and I will be naked when I die. The Lord gave these things to me, and He has taken them away. Praise the name of the Lord." In all this, Job did not sin or blame God"* (NCV).

- What do you think Job was focusing on when he chose to praise God during his great loss?
- What happens when you focus on your problems rather than the goodness of God?

Habakkuk 3:17-18: *"Even though the fig trees have no fruit and no grapes grow on the vines, even though the olive crop fails and the fields produce no grain, even though the sheep all die and the cattle stalls are empty, I'll still be joyful and glad because the Lord God is my Savior"* (GN).

- From Habakkuk 3:17-18, what is going on in Habakkuk's life?
- What did he choose to do, and how was that possible?
- What is the lesson to follow from this Scripture?

3. ASK GOD PASSIONATELY FOR WISDOM AND STRENGTH

Mike shares, "When you are hurt, you need wisdom and strength. Because you need to know what to do—that's wisdom, and you need the power to do it—that's strength.

- **Share your thoughts on this teaching.**

Job 12:13: *"True wisdom and real power belong to God; from Him, we learn how to live, and also what to live for"* (MSG).

- What does Job 12:13 mean to you?
- How would you apply this verse to your own life?

Psalm 37:39: *"The Lord saves good people; He is their strength in times of trouble"* (NCV).

- From Psalm 37:39, what words or ideas jump out to you about God?
- From Psalm 37:39, what can you expect from God when you come to Him in times of trouble?

Read the following scripture verses:

Psalm 3:5: *"I can lie down and go to sleep, and I'll wake up again because the Lord gives me strength"* (NCV).

1 Chronicles 16:11: *"Depend on the LORD and His strength; always go to Him for help"* (NCV)

- What is the common message in the above scriptures?

- What encourages you about the scriptures?
- What do you think will happen if you follow the key message from these Scriptures?

4. GATHER WITH OTHER BELIEVERS FOR SUPPORT

Mike shares: "When we get hurt, we naturally put up barriers and keep everybody at a big distance. Building walls and keeping people at a distance is a nice way to live a miserable life."

- Share your thoughts on this teaching.

Job 36:18-24: *(Elihu) "Don't let your anger and the pain you endured make you sneer at God. Your reputation and riches cannot protect you from distress, nor can you find safety in the dark world below. Be on guard! Don't turn to evil as a way of escape. God's power is unlimited. He needs no teachers to guide or correct Him. Others have praised God for what He has done, so join with them"* (CEV).

- From Job 36:18-24, what happens if you try to isolate yourself in your time of hardship?
- Why should you join other believers for worship instead?

Psalm 63:2: *"So here I am in the place of worship, eyes open, drinking in Your strength and glory"* (MSG).

- Based on Psalm 63:2, what do you think happens when you join other believers to worship?
- How does Psalm 63:2 encourage your commitment to your local Church?

5. KEEP ON PERSISTING

Job 2:9-10: *"Job's wife said to him, 'Are you still trying to maintain your integrity? Curse God and die.' But Job replied, 'You talk like a godless woman. Should we accept only good things from the hand of God and never anything bad?' So in all this, Job said nothing wrong"* (NLT).

- How does Job's persistence show up in the above Scripture?
- In what ways do you think society will try to oppose or distract you from trusting God in your time of hardship?

1 Peter 5:10: *"The God of all grace, who called you to His eternal glory in Christ, after you have suffered a little while, will Himself restore, support, and strengthen you, and He will place you on a firm foundation."*

- In 1 Peter 5:10, Paul says, the God of all grace will come to our defense in various ways in our time of suffering. What stands out to you most about this description?
- How does this verse encourage you to keep trusting God in your time of trouble?

SECTION 3: PERSONAL APPLICATION AND COMMITMENT

Be diligent in applying these principles: Tell God how you feel and ask Him to help you overcome any challenge. Praise Him amid your difficulties. Ask Him for His wisdom and strength. Gather with other believers for support and keep persisting.

D. PRAYER POINTS

1. Pray that you and the other members of your Small Group will respond positively to this message and will act on it.
2. Pray for a miraculous outcome as you and your group put this wisdom into practice.
3. Ask everyone in the group to share what they need prayer for, and then pray for those requests.
4. Request that one of your members lead in a closing prayer.

PLEASE REACH OUT TO ANYONE WHO DID NOT
MAKE IT TO YOUR MEETING

Part Two:
Small Group Guidelines and Helpful Hints for Hosts

Small Group Guidelines

Communicating shared values, expectations, and commitments is a good idea for every group. Such guidelines will help avoid unspoken agendas and unmet expectations. Please discuss these guidelines during Session One to lay the foundation for a healthy group experience. Feel free to modify anything that does not work for your group.

Clear Purpose: To grow healthy spiritual lives by building a healthy small group community.

Group Attendance: To give priority to the group meeting. Call or text if I won't be present or late for a meeting.

Safe Environment: To create a safe place where people can be heard and feel loved (no quick answers, snap judgments, or simple fixes, no politics, no controversial topics, and no selling products or services to other members).

Be Confidential: To keep anything that is shared strictly confidential. What is shared in the group stays in the group.

Conflict Resolution: To avoid gossip and to immediately resolve any concerns by following the principles of Matthew 18:15-17.

Spiritual Health: To give group members the opportunity to support and help me live a healthy, balanced life that pleases God. Please take what is helpful from the group discussions, consistent with the Word of God. Not every member's comment will be biblical, so don't be offended by unbiblical opinions. Stick with what is biblical.

Limit Our Freedom: Limit our freedom by not serving or consuming alcohol during small group meetings or events to avoid causing a weaker brother or sister to stumble (1 Corinthians 8:1-13; Romans 14:19-21).

Welcome Newcomers: To invite our friends who might benefit from this study and warmly welcome newcomers.

Building Relationships: To get to know other group members and pray for them regularly.

Shared Responsibility: Every small group member can help share the responsibilities of the group's study (e.g., Facilitate discussions, host or co-host meetings, lead in prayer, etc.)

Meeting Day:

_____

Starting & Ending Time:

_____

Meeting Location:

_____

Helpful Tips for Small Group Hosts

Congratulations! Accepting the responsibility of leading a small group means you are joining Jesus in His role as a shepherd. Here are some things to consider as you prepare to lead your group, whether for one meeting or the entire series. Know that you have the support of many people. Though you may not feel qualified to lead this group, God has appointed you to do so and promised that "He will never leave or abandon you" (Hebrews 13:5). You will be blessed as you serve God and His people.

Be friendly and be yourself. God wants to use your unique gifts and temperament. Be sure to greet people as they come in with a warm smile. This can set the tone for the gathering. Remember, they are taking a big step by showing up. Admit when you don't have an answer and apologize when you make a mistake. Your group will appreciate you for it

Prepare for your meeting ahead of time. Take some time before the meeting and go over the discussion points. Make a note of your responses. For most groups, there are too many questions in each discussion guide chapter to cover in one session. After considering the needs of your group, you may choose to select a few questions from each section.

When you ask a question, be patient. Do not preach. Someone will eventually respond. Sometimes people need a moment or two of silence to think about the question or gather their thoughts before they speak. Avoid the urge to preach. A small group is a discussion-based Bible study. After someone responds, affirm their response with a simple "thanks" or "great answer." Then ask, "How about somebody else?" or "Would someone who hasn't shared like to add anything?" Be sensitive to members who are hesitant to say, pray, or do anything. They will blossom over time if you provide a safe, friendly environment. Let everyone know they are loved and appreciated and that the group would value their input.

Provide transitions between questions. Ask if anyone would like to read the Bible passage, paragraph, or question, perhaps someone who hasn't already. Try not to call on anyone; instead, ask for a volunteer and wait until someone starts. Make a point of thanking the person who reads aloud. Find gentle ways to quiet or refocus overbearing people who speak all the time so others can speak up. Say something like, "Let's give someone who hasn't shared the opportunity to read the next point or question or perhaps share their thoughts."

Pray for your group members by name. Before getting started, pray for the meeting and its attendees. Praying for one another can alter the dynamic of any group. Pray that God would use your time together to speak to the hearts of those who are participating. When something in your group meetings calls for prayer, take a moment to pray as a group before moving forward. Be sensitive to the direction of the Spirit. Set the group on a prayer foundation.

Don't try to do it alone. Even if you have the ability to host every time, it is better for the spiritual development of the group if you rotate hosting duties. As a result, it may be a good idea to find a co-leader and switch facilitators occasionally. Jesus often had his followers go into ministry in pairs (Luke 10:1). This will lighten your load and boost morale in the group. It's as simple as asking for assistance.

You'll be surprised at the response.

Respect people's time. Begin and end on time. Set clear expectations and do your best to stick to them.

Have fun. Laugh. Create an enjoyable, memorable environment. The Bible says, *"A cheerful heart is good medicine"* (Proverbs 17:22 NIV). Don't be too rigid. Give space for engagement and Christian relationships to form.

Read the following Scriptures as a devotional exercise before your first opportunity to lead to help prepare you with a shepherd's heart. Trust me on this one. If you do this, you will be more than ready for your meeting.

"When Jesus saw the crowds, He had compassion on them because they were harassed and helpless, like sheep without a shepherd. Then He said to His disciples, "The harvest is plentiful, but the workers are few. Ask the Lord of the harvest, therefore, to send out workers into His harvest field" (Matthew 9:36-38 NIV)

"I am the good shepherd; I know my sheep and my sheep know me— just as the Father knows me and I know the Father—and I lay down my life for the sheep" (John 10:14-15 NIV)

"Be shepherds of God's flock that is under your care, watching over them—not because you must, but because you are willing, as God wants you to be; not pursuing dishonest gain, but eager to serve; not lording it over those entrusted to you, but being examples to the flock. And when the Chief Shepherd appears, you will receive the crown of glory that will never fade away" (1 Peter 5:2-4 NIV)

"Therefore if you have any encouragement from being united with Christ, if any comfort from his love, if any common sharing in the Spirit, if any tenderness and compassion, then make my joy complete by being like-minded,

having the same love, being one in spirit and of one mind. Do nothing out of selfish ambition or vain conceit. Rather, in humility, value others above yourselves, not looking to your own interests but each of you to the interests of the others. In your relationships with one another, have the same mindset as Christ Jesus" (Philippians 2:1-5 NIV)

"Let us hold unswervingly to the hope we profess, for He who promised is faithful. And let us consider how we may spur one another on toward love and good deeds, not giving up meeting together, as some are in the habit of doing, but encouraging one another—and all the more as you see the Day approaching" (Hebrews 10:23-25 NIV)

"Just as a nursing mother cares for her children, so we cared for you. Because we loved you so much, we were delighted to share with you not only the gospel of God but our lives as well ... For you know that we dealt with each of you as a father deals with his own children, encouraging, comforting and urging you to live lives worthy of God, who calls you into His kingdom and glory" (1 Thessalonians 2:7-8, 11-12 NIV)

My Small Group Rooster

NAME	PHONE NUMBER	E-MAIL

Inspired by what you just heard?
Connect with Mike Prah

Check out the following resources for spiritual guidance and inspiration at www.mikeprah.com.

- Video Teachings
- Bible Study content
- Podcasts
- Book excerpts
- Blogs, Journals, and Articles
- First look at upcoming books
- Downloadable content
- Online store where you can buy books, merchandise, and special offers.

For more information or to book Mike for a speaking engagement, please email Mike Prah at mike@mikeprah.com

Additional Notes

Additional Notes

Additional Notes